Christy Lane's

ALL THAT JAZZ AND MORE...

The Complete Book of Jazz Dancing
Second Edition

 KENDALL/HUNT PUBLISHING COMPANY
4050 Westmark Drive   Dubuque, Iowa 52002

A publication of
Let's Do It! Productions
P.O. Box 5483 Spokane, WA 99205
Copyright ® 1994 LDI Productions
All rights reserved. Printed in the U.S.A.

Library of Congress Catalog Card Number: 93-061401

ISBN: 0-8403-9020-3

Photography: Pete Moroz
Edited by: Rebekah Angus

First Edition 1983 by Leisure Press

Printed in the United States of America
10 9 8 7 6 5 4 3 2 1

CONTENTS

ACKNOWLEDGEMENTS

I am indebted to all the students and teachers for their inspiration to compel me to write this book. Their questions and encouragement are a constant motivation for me.

INTRODUCTION

It was eighteen years ago that I received my first letter of inquiry from a desperate jazz dance instructor pleading for literature on the subject of jazz dance. From that time on, I began traveling nationally and the letters continued to come. Where did I get my material? What is the basic technique and how can I teach the progressions? These inquiries plus my own curiosity encouraged me to seek a universal technique and approach to studying and teaching jazz dance. My ambition was not to become a professional performing dancer, but rather to learn more about the art form that I came to love. My enjoyment and satisfaction in teaching have led me to these findings of sound jazz dance technique.

I have had the fortunate opportunity to travel in 48 states teaching and training at workshops. During my travels I searched for common denominators in instruction that would meet the needs of students and teachers alike. From New York to Los Angeles I saw many very different styles, techniques, and philosophies, not only in private dance studios, but in private gymnastics clubs, high schools, colleges, universities, YMCAs, dance conventions, and competitions.

One thing was obvious wherever I went, jazz dancing could turn an empty room into excitement, energy, and beauty.

This study is the product of extensive research in the field, from writings, films, videos, classes taken from masters, observation of professional choreographers as well as my own classes including the special master workshops where many techniques were tested. I have written this book in an attempt to standardize the basics. The arrangement is unique in that it is designed for the novice as well as the advanced. It will be an asset to anyone involved in jazz dance today, whether a dancer, teacher, choreographer, actor or actress, athlete, or aerobics fan—there's something here for you. Let us not exclude the physical education instructors who are dedicating so much of their effort and time building programs in their schools and keeping up with the demands of dance in the curriculum. This book is especially for those teachers in the educational setting.

Whatever your interest or perspective, I invite you to join me in the exciting adventure of **jazz dance.**

1 JAZZ DANCE TODAY

Welcome to the world of jazz dance! Whether you are a novice student, an advanced student, or especially if you are a teacher, this book is designed to inform you, stimulate you, enhance your technique, and improve your control in the wonderful art of jazz dance.

When you think of jazz you probably think of Fred Astaire or Gene Kelly dancing in the thirties. Perhaps the images of musical theater, the swing, lindy hop, movies, charleston, music television, Vegas shows, variety shows, or an opening of a television awards show comes to mind. The nineties, however, have produced much more. Jazz dance has now begun to regard itself as an art and is used as a means of communication. It is available through many venues of our culture—it is literally everywhere—in night club acts, sports entertainment, commercials, gymnastic routines, aerobic routines, and of course, the theater. No longer is it done exclusively to jazz music. It has permeated pop, rhythm, blues, rock, country, and funk as well. Never has jazz dance been so popular as today. Everywhere people are gathering in classes in increasing numbers. Fun, excitement, challenge, entertainment, fitness, sport, social, artistic, and self-expression are all descriptions of jazz dance.

Why is it so popular? Aside from the media influence and pure enjoyment, jazz dance is a natural form of dance that is freer, more exciting, more rhythmic, and less classical than other dance styles. This dance form teaches the body to move rhythmically while challenging the mind with patterned movement. It can develop muscle tone, reduce fatigue, release tension psychologically and build self-confidence by giving you a feeling of control over your body. It is an aesthetically beautiful and creative art form. Perhaps

1

the best thing about jazz dance is that it is contemporary.

The integration of other disciplines of dance have created the versatile jazz that is seen today. During the past decade jazz has adapted material from artistic, social, and theatrical dance forms. For example, ballet has contributed to jazz by giving it exactness and alignment. The influence of modern dance has given it greater use of the torso, natural expressiveness and more fluidity. Tap dance has brought rhythmic movement, terminology, and speed. Gymnastics has provided flexibility, suppleness, and strength. From folk, ballroom, and social dance we see step patterns, and character dance provides versatility. We are now seeing many cultural influences and, of course, contemporary dances such as funk, street, and rock, which have stimulated jazz with progressive styles that utilize a variety of movements of the hips and torso.

It is apparent that these many influences have shaped the jazz of today. Jazz has developed many styles, that if named could be categorized as follows: Ballet Jazz (a lyrical style with many ballet movements), Modern Jazz (more fluid style with greater torso movement), Rock or Street Jazz (current contemporary dances intertwined with jazz technique), Broadway Musical Jazz (musical show production dancing), Afro-Jazz (jazz influenced with African cultural movements), and Latin Jazz (emphasis on hip movements and a 1-2-3 rhythm).

Now let's turn to jazz dance and its value to you, the reader. As you read this book, you will explore jazz technique and terminology that is used in all of the above mentioned styles of jazz. As you progress in developing your skills in jazz, it is very important to supplement your training with classes in ballet, modern dance, social dance, gymnastics and cultural movements. It is beyond the scope of this book to define every one of these dance forms. We will, however, use some of the terms and movements from basic beginning ballet.

From Los Angeles to New York, there are many different performers and teachers with their own backgrounds, all putting forth their own techniques. Through this influence, a universal technique—a common denominator—has emerged. You are about to learn this universal technique.

2 THE JAZZ CLASS

Let's Get Ready

It seems we have accepted ideas for dance technique based on traditions developed hundreds of years ago. During that time art was likely to be ritualistic and geometric rather than realistic or humanistic. As society's awareness of the anatomical and kinesiological parameters of the human body has increased, jazz classes have changed to accommodate the needs and demands of the human body. It's wonderful that with the recent fitness explosion has come concern for the personal safety of the dancer and more realistic approaches to dance.

Today, teachers and dancers are placing a greater emphasis on exercise techniques designed to develop control, muscular strength, flexibility, and coordination of all body parts. Thus, dancers are more effective and seem to have fewer injuries. Rather than just developing the "lines" of a dancer, as was once done, individuals are now concerned with training a dancer's body until it becomes completely and instantly responsive like a fine-tuned instrument.

From east to west, the jazz dance class still follows basically the same format as the traditional ballet class, 1) *warm up and center floor exercise technique* for conditioning and control, 2) *locomotive movement* technique for balance and movement through space, and 3) *combinations* or choreographed routines. In a professional studio, the average <u>minimum</u> amount of class time is one hour for beginners and one and one-half hours for advanced students. However, time allotments for each section (technique, locomotor movement, and routines) vary with each class. For example, a teacher may want to spend more

3

Jazz Dance Class

15 Min.   ## Warm Up
Increase Body Temperature
Flexibility and Strength Technique
Isolation Technique

10 Min.   ## Center Floor Exercise Techniques
Kicks
Turns

10 Min.   ## Locomotive Moves
Walks
Traveling Steps
Leaps and Jumps
Floorwork

20 Min.   ## Combinations

5 Min.   ## Cool Down

time on technique at the beginning of the term and more time on combinations when getting close to performance time. More recently, studio work also includes a brief "warm down" consisting of stretches, deep breathing, or a slow routine.

The class format on page 4 was designed after extensive research in numerous dance studios throughout the country as well as following current scientific guidelines for human movement. If you are a teacher, the percentage of time spent on each section in relationship to the entire class can be adjusted to the total time allotted for the entire series of classes. Since this format was designed for an hour class, you can increase or decrease each section proportionally (for example, forty-five minute classes or one and one-half hour classes.) This class structure also can be adapted for younger students as well as adults. By simplifying the movements and applying more repetition of techniques (and more "play"), younger students can readily benefit from this format.

Each section will be presented in this book for the beginning, low-intermediate, high-intermediate, and advanced levels. Please note that certain baseline levels of flexibility, strength, coordination, timing, and fundamental skills are necessary before a student can approach skills at the advanced level. (For example, you cannot do a split-split leap without the strength to jump and flexibility to do the splits.) The progressions from Levels 1-4 should assist you in this matter.

Pay special attention to the technique sections. Acquiring a sound technique is an investment in the future. Adherence to sound techniques frees your body to reach your ultimate potential. Once you have acquired the techniques, you are ready to find the most exciting part of dancing—developing your own style.

What to Wear

Proper attire is necessary in dance. There are many wonderful products on the market today and these are readily available at dance store outlets and department stores. However, some can be extremely expensive, particularly when compared to their usefulness. Here is a simplified guide that hopefully will be beneficial to you on your next shopping spree.

Shoes. Light weight soft leather (jazz) shoes or boots are best for dancing jazz because they allow your feet to both breathe and be mobile. The soles should have enough friction to let you move safely. The best type of floors to dance on are wood floors with very little floor treatment. Be extremely cautious of waxed floors. (Since I cannot control the floor surface, I bring a set of three shoes to every new class I enroll in: one with leather bottoms in case the studio floor has a thin rubber on the surface called "marlee", one with a very, very fine light rubber sole, and the other with a thick rubber sole. I use the thick rubber sole shoes on extremely slippery waxed or dirty floors.) Check the floor surface at the studio you are attending before purchasing new jazz shoes. Most jazz shoes on the market today are expensive and should be purchased only if you are a serious student. They come in canvas and leather, the latter being the most advantageous since the more you wear them, the more they conform to your foot (purchase a snug fitting pair since they stretch). If you are a beginner, or teach in a low-income community, light-weight tennis shoes (sneakers) may be the shoe for you temporarily.

Try to avoid heels if at all possible. Heels have the same effect as street shoes with heels. (They shorten the achilles and put pressure on the small of your back). Most dancers who are required to perform in shoes with heels will need to practice with them because their motion "center" (See Warm Up Chapter) will be different. If you must wear them, make sure your ankles and legs are in good condition and always stretch your calves before and after dancing. It is essential to perform the floor technique exercises in this book without shoes or with a very flexible jazz shoe so your feet have a full range of motion and good articulation.

Some dancers prefer dancing entirely barefoot, but the lack of shoes is limiting on turns and does not offer foot support. Never dance in full tights without shoes. If your tights are not the stirrup type, cut the toes and heels out of your tights. Then you can put nylon socks over your feet before putting on your shoes. Avoid wearing socks alone as footwear because they are slippery and dangerous.

Leotards. Leotard (the close fitting garment that extends from your neck to groin area) designs for men and women are too numerous to mention in this book. However, I recommend that you try the leotards on your body because some brand names run smaller than they are marked. Be sure the material breathes—cotton is the best. Higher cut legs give the appearance of longer legs. A unitard is a one piece leotard and pant outfit combining the effect of leotard and tights.

Tights. Tights are close fitting coverings over your legs. They are available in various sizes and colors. The choice is simply personal preference. Always try them on. If they fit snugly purchase the next largest size. Tights, like all dance wear, should be laundered in cold water and hung to dry because they tend to lose their elasticity when exposed to high temperatures. You might also want to check with you local dance studio for a possible color code.

Jazz Pants/Shorts. Jazz pants/shorts can also be considered optional dance attire. Again, they should stretch, breathe easily, and fit close to the body so your body image is easy to see. They are usually worn over tights, but that is a preference. Jazz pants can be purchased with flared or straight legs. The plastic baggie pants on the market today are not recommended. Not only do they inhibit your ability to see your body alignment, but more importantly they prevent your body from cooling through evaporation. It is not only dangerous to lose large quantities of body fluid, but is almost totally worthless as a weight-loss technique because of the natural replacement of fluids.

Leg Warmers. The purpose of leg warmers is to keep your muscles warm during breaks in dancing because there is a great deal of stop and go motion in a jazz class. However, since there is some controversy on their value, they should be considered optional attire.

Sweatshirts. This item is a good investment to avoid chills after workouts. Refrain from wearing them during class once your body is sufficiently warmed up since they greatly reduce the ability to see your body perform.

Dance Belt and Bra. A male dance belt and a female dance bra add support and provide a desirable appearance. Both are recommended.

Knee Pads. The same style of pads used by other athletes. Lighter weight ones look better and are more versatile in dancing. Keep them in your dance bag in case a teacher's choreography requires floorwork.

Water Bottle. A great way to avoid fatigue. An accidental spill may not ruin the dance floor! Always bring one to class. Stay hydrated.

Now, let's dance!

3 Basic Jazz Positions

The following positions and terms are the most common for jazz dance. Become familiar with the following terms because they will be used throughout the book. It is recommended that you assume the position and go through each movement as the description is read. Some basic modern and ballet terms frequently used in jazz dance are listed in this section.

Foot Positions

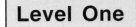

Jazz First Position.   Your feet are parallel, about one to two inches apart.

Jazz Second Position.   Your feet are parallel, approximately shoulder width apart.

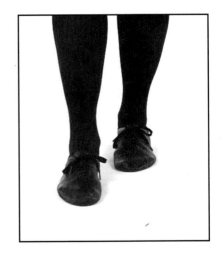

Jazz Fourth Position.   Your feet are parallel separated approximately twelve inches apart with one foot in front of the other.

Jazz Fifth Position.   Your feet are parallel with the heel of one foot in line with the toe of the other foot.

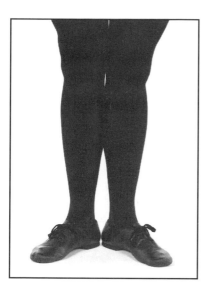

Ballet First Position. Your heels are together and your legs rotated outward from your hips. *Note:* Do not force a 180° turnout. Only turn out to the point where it feels comfortable and secure and can be maintained without disturbing your body alignment.

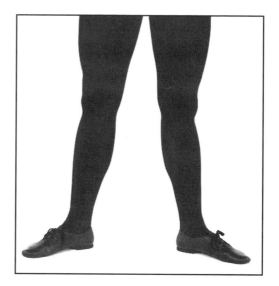

Ballet Second Position. Your legs are turned out from your hips, your heels are approximately twelve inches apart.

Ballet Fourth Position. Your legs are turned out from your hips with one foot directly in front of the other.

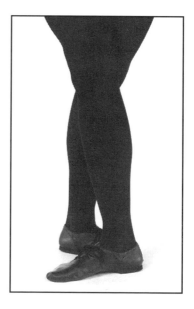

Ballet Fifth Position. Same as ballet fourth position, only with the heel of your front foot placed at the joint of the toes of your back foot.

Arm Positions

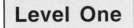

Level One

Jazz First Position.   Your elbows are straight with your arms down and slightly outward from body. Turn your palms inward.

Jazz Second Position.   Your elbows are lifted and your arms held horizontal with your palms down and your arms slightly in front of your shoulders. (Note: Feel the shoulders pressing down and the carriage of the arms from the upper back.)

Jazz Third Position.   One arm is extended over your head with your other arm in a jazz second position. (Note: Arms may vary according to what ballet style your studio teaches).

Jazz Fourth Position. Either arm may be high. The raised arm has an outward palm and the other arm is slightly below the ribs with palm facing downward.

Jazz High Fifth Position. Your arms are overhead but angled slightly outward from your body with your palms inward or outward in a high "V" position.

Jazz Low Fifth Position. Arms form a circle slightly below your rib cage. (Note: The feeling is like you are holding a large beach ball).

Jazz Diagonal Arms. One arm is overhead and slightly outward with your palm out. The other arm is down and slightly outward with your palm in. (Note: Your arms should form a straight line.)

Ballet First Position. Your arms are slightly curved and downward. Your palms face your body.

Ballet Second Position. Your arms are open to your side with a slight curve downward. Three-quarter of each palm is held open to the front.

Ballet Third Position. Either arm may be high. The other arm is in the second position. (This is also known as fourth position in some ballet schools.)

Ballet Fourth Position. Either arm may be high. The raised arm forms a half-circle above your head. The other arm forms a half-circle slightly lower than your rib cage.

Ballet Fifth Position En Haut.   Your arms form a circle above your head.

Ballet Fifth Position En Avant.   Your arms form a circle in front of your body with your hands only a few inches apart and your palms facing each other.

Hand Positions

Level One

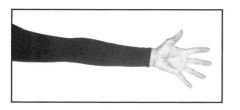

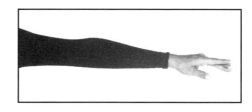

Jazz Palms.   Your fingers are spread and fully extended with your hands in a plane surface.

Jazz Hands.   Your palms face downward with your fingers and hands in a relaxed position.

Body Positions

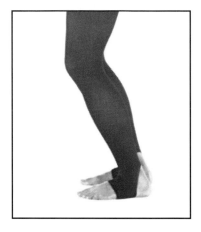

Plié (ple a).   A position or a movement referring to lowering the level of your body by bending your knees. On a **demi-plié** your heels do not rise off the floor as you lower. Instead press your heels into the floor, which will cause your achilles tendon to stretch. A **grand plié** occurs after a demi-plié position and allows your heels to lift, except in second position when your heels remain on the floor.

Relevé (reh leh va).   Rise to the ball of your foot (or both feet).

Plié-Relevé Position.   Standard combination position used quite often in jazz. Bend the knees at the same time you rise to the ball of your feet.

Turned In   Turned Out

Passé (pah say).   Bent knee lifted, toes to opposite knee. The toes of your free leg touch the inside of your supporting knee. The parallel passé is executed with one knee forward. The foot position varies on an outward passé from the lower calf to the knee.

Tendu (tahn dew).   To point the foot with the foot never leaving the floor. The whole foot slides from first or fifth position to the front, side, or back. This exercise strengthens the foot by alternating tension and relaxation as it is moved along the floor.

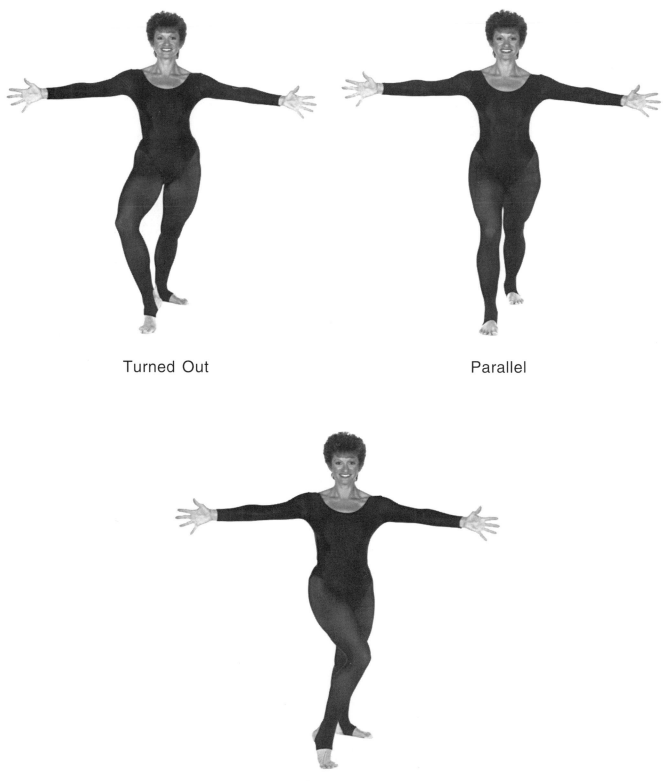

Turned Out   Parallel

Turned In

Forward Lunge.   With either leg straight, your other leg is bent after a forward stepping motion.

Turned Out

Parallel

Turned In

Side Lunge.   Same as a forward lunge only performed in second position.

Back Arch   Side Arch

Body Arch. Curve your entire body in a given direction.

Contraction. An upper body contraction occurs as you contract your chest and abdominal muscles. A lower body contraction consists of tilting your pelvic area.

Level Two

Jazz Split.   Your back leg is bent and your front leg is straight in a hurdle sitting position.

Swastika (swa stik a).   Both knees are bent under your body. Arm position is optional.

Développé (deh veh loh pay).   Your leg is "developed" from a bent knee position to a straight leg position.

Body Wave (or Roll).   Occurs from your feet up to your head. Begin in a demi-plié position. Roll your knees forward first, then your hips, chest, arms, and head.

Arabesque (air a besk).   Your body is balanced over one foot with your other leg fully extended either on the ground or lifted. Your arms can be in a variety of positions.

Back Attitude   Front Attitude

Attitude.   A pose on one leg with your other leg lifted and bent at the knee. The knee of your lifted leg should be at the same height or higher than the foot.

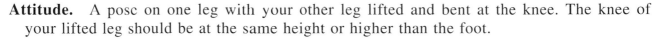

Level Three

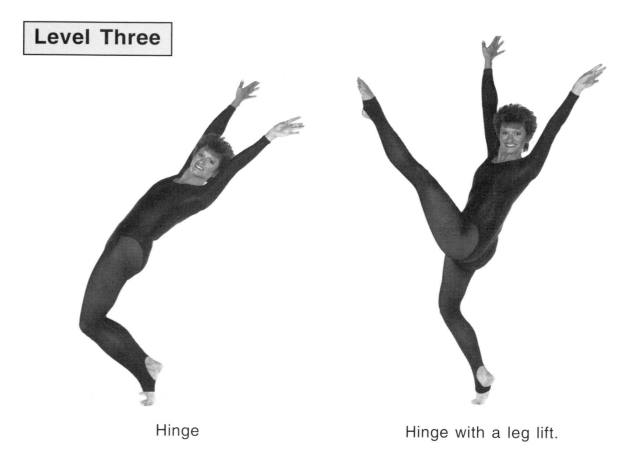

Hinge   Hinge with a leg lift.

Hinge.   Lean backward with a straight back in plié-relevé position.

Swastika with a Pelvic Lift.   Begin in a swastika position. Lift the hips up using one arm for support. Perform with caution if you have knee problems.

Side Splits

Second Position Splits

Splits.   180° split of the legs. In the side splits, the front knee should be pointed straight up or turned out. If you turn the front leg out it must be turned out from the hip, not the knee. The back knee should be facing the side. Only face the knee downward if you are advanced and do not have knee problems.

Level Four

Front Layover

Side Layover

Tabletop Layover

Back Layover

Layovers.   A balancing position on one leg. (See Strength Exercise Technique in the Warm Up Chapter).

4 THE WARM UP

The Center

Good posture and alignment are extremely beneficial and necessary in jazz dance. Without proper alignment you may not be strengthening or stretching the desired muscles or you may be limiting yourself in executing dance movements. Most importantly, improper alignment may make you susceptible to injury, especially in the back region. For balance, for safety, for turns, and for control, good posture is essential.

For proper posture, some thoughts to remember are to:

- Imagine yourself in between two sheets of glass.

- Hold your spine straight by lengthening your vertebrae.

- Keep your neck free from tension by relaxing your shoulders.

- Lift your rib cage up and in.

- Lift your stomach by feeling your stomach muscles both pulling toward your back and lifting directly under your rib cage.

- Your pelvis should be straight, neither dropped forward nor tucked under. When

your pelvis is incorrectly tilted forward, the weight of your upper body is carried in front of the legs—an alignment which can cause lower back strain. Because of the stress an incorrect alignment places on your back you should be particularly careful to ensure that you assume the proper position at all times.

When your body is correctly held and balanced it is called your body's "center" or being centered. You should always be feeling at your center throughout your dancing because it is a source of control, especially while in turning. Stop . . . close your eyes and feel this position. Now with your eyes closed, visualize your upper body continuing to grow while at the same time imagining "pressing" into the ground. This lengthening process will teach you the lift and stretch that is so important in dance.

Flexibility Exercise Technique

It is necessary to stretch your body through a full range of motion before you dance. Unique to many sports, dance skills require a full range of motion. If you feel your class is not giving you a sufficient warm-up, it is necessary for you to stretch on your own *before* class. Only *you* know your body.

The most ideal type of jazz class is one that begins with a 5 minute warm-up that includes any type of aerobic movement to increase body temperature before you begin your stretching exercises. Ideas for this warm-up could include performing basic funk/rock steps nonstop. Another idea is to walk, skip, or chassé (see Locomotor Movement Chapter) around the room utilizing the arms. Any aerobic dance movement would be beneficial.

Beginning Stretch—Solo

sides

upper back

neck

shoulders

chest/shoulders

calves

calves

quadriceps

groin

hips

back

hip flexors

hamstrings

low back/hips

back/chest

overall

Intermediate Stretch–Solo

sides

neck

upper back

shoulders

triceps

calves

calves

hip flexors

hip flexors

back

calves

quadriceps

buttocks

groin

sides

back/hamstrings

adductors

back

hips

hamstrings

chest

overall

Advanced Stretch–Solo

sides

shoulders

neck

upper back

spine back

shoulders/arms

low back/chest

calves

hip flexors

quadriceps

hamstrings

groin

sides/hamstrings

adductors

hips/buttocks

hips/buttocks

hamstrings

hips/low back

overall

recover/relax

overall

Beginning Stretch–Partner

sides

neck

shoulders/chest

calves

hip flexors/chest

groin/adductors

buttocks/hips

back

hamstrings

lower back/hips

quadriceps/hip flexors

hip flexor/quadriceps

lower body

upper body

Intermediate Stretch–Partner

sides

back

neck

shoulders/chest

hip flexors

calves

calves

groin/adductors

adductors

back

hamstrings

buttocks/hips

quadriceps

upper body

Advanced Stretch–Partner

sides

shoulders

hip flexors

hamstrings

quadriceps

shoulders

adductors

hamstring/back

groin

hips

hamstrings

buttocks/low back

front

adductors

hamstrings

If you are a teacher, using fun and relative music is a great way to get dancers involved in the class from a motivational and psychological stand point.

After your body is sufficiently warmed, stretch correctly to prepare it for class. Be sure that your stretch routine includes the major muscle groups illustrated and hold the stretches for at least ten seconds. Remember, to increase flexibility, hold the stretches for thirty to sixty seconds *at the end* of your class. (See Stretch-a-b-i-l-i-t-y Chapter).

Partner exercises are a pleasant way to add variety because the stretches allow you to completely relax while undertaking each exercise. Dancers need to communicate clearly before they reach the point of pain.

These stretching exercises can be performed one right after another to motivating and/or relaxing music. Teachers should add to the stretch routine any other dance body movements that you will be utilizing during your routine. Go through the techniques you are about to teach slowly through range of motion, then increase the speed. For example if you are including an attitude in your combination, perform the attitude slowly on the floor first.

Common in the center floor technique section of classes today is a routine called an "adage" (ah dodge). In adage teachers choreograph a standardized slow series of center floor movements. These movements are performed as though without effort, but are a definite test of balance, control, strength, and movement memory. Adage allows dancers to memorize the movements, thus requiring less concentration on succeeding movements, and more concentration on placement, corrections, and "dancing" the exercise. It also allows the teacher to point out certain errors and achievements without stopping the music. It is essential to vary the routine because the same exercises may limit the areas of the body being worked as well as becoming boring for both students and teacher. In order to put together your own routine try combining the exercises illustrated in this chapter.

As you perform the stretching exercises, mentally reach beyond your physical capability—always stretching. Try to become aware of every part of your body. Feel and look alert. Your body can express energy just by the way you hold yourself. And lastly, enjoy!

Strength Exercise Technique

For better performance and control, strength is a vital ingredient. Balancing your strength and flexibility decreases injury, increases performance potential and heightens body tone. For a muscle to become stronger, it must be worked for increasingly longer periods of time, worked more frequently, or worked with increased intensity.

Make sure the following exercises are included in your strength workout to insure balanced muscles and adequate strength. Modify the exercises to fit your style and music. Listed also are some guidelines for the number of repetitions. To determine the number for you, work to, but not beyond your fatigue level. Increase the number of repetitions to build up to each successful level gradually. As you advance, supplement your dance class with outside training.

Pelvic Control and Abdominal Strength

Pelvic Tilt

Level 1. Lie in a supine (on your back) position. Keep your knees up and your arms out to the side. Press the small of your back into the floor. Hold for eight counts, continuing to breathe normally. Relax.

Level 2. Do the above with legs straight.

Level 3. From a sitting position contract your lower back. Lift your chest slowly as you straighten your back. Reach forward with a flat back. Bring your arms to fifth position. Return to a sitting position with your arms in second position.

Stomach Curls

Note: Your stomach muscles are your best protection for proper pelvic alignment. Weak abdominal muscles can cause forward pelvic tilt which can lead to small back problems.

Level 1. Lie in a supine position with your knees bent. Place your hands on your knees and curl your trunk up until your fingertips touch the top of your knees. Roll down slowly, taking eight counts. Repeat ten times. Then place your hands behind your head and curl to each side at least ten times each.

Level 2. Repeat the above twenty times.

Level 3. Repeat the above forty times.

Level 4. Repeat the above fifty or more times.

Stomach Twist

Level 1.   From a supine position with your knees bent, drop your knees to the right. Use abdominal contraction to initiate bringing the knees back up to a vertical position. Repeat to the left. Repeat eight times on each side.

Level 2.   Do the above with feet off the floor. Repeat eight times in each direction.

Level 3.   Repeat the above sixteen times on each side.

Level 4.   Repeat the above twenty-five times on each side.

Calf Strength

Calf Raises

Level 1.   Begin in jazz first position. Rise up and down on your toes three times. Hold the last time for eight counts in relevé position. Keep your heels parallel and your weight centered on the balls of your feet.

Level 2.   Repeat the above eight times and use choreographed continuous arm movements on the last hold position.

Level 3.   Same as Level 1 only rise up and down on the toes of one foot only with the non-supporting leg in passé position.

Side Strength

Side Reach

Level 1.   From a standing second position, place your arms in high fifth position. Stretch over to the side for four counts and slowly return to center. Repeat with your other side.

Level 2.   Perform the above from a sitting straddle position keeping your knees facing directly upward.

Leg and Buttock Strength

Note: See also Kick Chapter for more leg strength exercises.

Pliés

Level 1. Demi-plié in jazz first position twice. Repeat in jazz second and fourth and ballet first, second, fourth and fifth positions.

Level 2. Perform the above, only add a grande plié to each position. *Note:* If done correctly, pliés can stretch some of the muscles of your thighs, such as the adductor, and can strengthen some muscles, such as the hamstrings and quadriceps. Skeletal joint range is probably increased. If pliés are performed incorrectly, they will probably do more damage than good. Avoid grande pliés if you have knee problems of any type.

Level 3. Demi-plié, as illustrated above, in jazz first position. Lift your heels keeping your knees bent. Straighten your legs, then lower your heels. Reverse. Begin with a relevé. Demi-plié with your heels still lifted. Place your heels down, then straighten your legs. Repeat in all of the foot positions.

Leg Extensions

Level 1.   In the jazz first position with the second position jazz palms point your foot as you passé forward and bend your elbows in. Développé with flexed foot forward as your palms go forward. Return to the passé position with your elbows in. Return to the first position and repeat with the other leg. Repeat the above only développé your foot to second position instead of forward. Keep your knee up or turned out. Repeat again, only développé your foot to the back keeping your knee towards the floor. *Note:* Each movement in this series is performed in two counts.

Level 2.   Passé forward. Flex your foot as your leg développés forward. Rotate your leg to the side while keeping your hip down. Return to forward passé. Repeat, bringing your leg from the second développé to the front. Repeat, bringing your leg from the back to the side. Repeat all motions with your other leg.

Level 3.   All of the aforementioned, only relevé when performing all the développé motions.

Layovers (See illustrations on page 23)

Note: Due to the strength and flexibility needed to perform a layover, all layovers are considered a Level 4. Imagine somebody grabbing your heel and another person grabbing your arms, each pulling in opposite directions. This stretching effect will help you maintain your balance.

Level 4.   Passé forward in jazz first position. Flex foot as you développé front. Rotate your leg to the side. Bend your trunk forward from your waist with a flat back and rotate your knee with the trunk. Hold. Return to the upright position. Return to the passé. Return to first position. Repeat with your other leg. This is known as a tabletop layover.

Level 4.   Passé in jazz first position. Développé with a flexed foot forward. Bring your trunk back with a flat back reaching your arms forward. Hold. Return your trunk, keeping your leg at the same height. Passé and return. Repeat with your other leg. This is a back layover.

Level 4. In jazz first position, passé your foot forward. Développé your flexed foot forward. Rotate your leg to the side. Stretch your trunk and arms to the opposite side. Hold. Return your trunk. Return to passé. Return to first position and repeat with your other leg. This is a side layover.

Level 4. Passé in jazz first position. Développé your flexed foot to the side. Rotate your leg to the back. Bring your trunk forward and stretch into a scale. Return your trunk. Passé forward. Return to the first position. Repeat with your other leg. This is a front layover.

Level 4. Variation. All of the above layovers are performed in relevé when executing the layover portion of the exercise.

Hip Lift

Level 1. In a supine position bend your knees with your feet flat on the floor and your arms to the side. Lift your pelvis by tilting your pelvis backward for eight counts. Hold that position for eight counts, then slowly lower yourself by rolling your back onto the ground feeling each vertebrae.

Level 2. Same as above, but only instead of holding the lifted position, alternate lifting your hips for four counts each. Reduce to two counts, then to one count.

Level 3. Perform the pelvic tilt exercise, only développé one leg up when your pelvis is lifted. Reverse with other leg.

Straddle Hold

Level 1. In a straddle position gradually move your trunk forward in a flat back position with your arms in second position. Only go to the point of control even if it is a small distance. Hold. Return and repeat four times.

Level 2.   In a straddle position move your trunk forward as far as possible without the support of your hands, then place your hands and stretch with a round back. Slowly reach out to a flat back position and return to a sitting position. Repeat four times.

Level 3.   In a straddle position, with your arms overhead and without the support of your hands, move your trunk forward as far as possible. Return to an upright position. Repeat eight times.

Level 4.   Perform the above, only instead of moving your trunk forward, rotate the trunk side, front, side, then back to the original position.

Hinge

Level 1.   In a kneeling position with your knees approximately twelve inches apart, hinge backwards by lowering as far as possible while maintaining a flat back position. Return to an upright position.

Level 2.   Same as Level 1, only after you reach the hinge position, contract and release pelvic area twice before returning to an upright position.

Level 3.   Hinge back as far as possible, then contract the pelvic area. Arch your back and swing arms back as you execute a wave through the body to an upright position.

Level 4.   Stand in jazz first position holding onto a ballet barre or chair. Plié relevé as you hinge back with a straight back. Free arm goes to the high diagonal. Hold for two counts. Swing arm through to a body wave and return to jazz first position on relevé. Hold for two counts, then lower heels.

Back Strength

Back Extensions

Level 1. Begin in a prone position (on your stomach) with your arms stretched over your head. Lift and stretch your right arm off the ground a few inches from the floor. At the same time lift and hold your left leg off the ground. Hold for eight counts. Repeat on your other side.

Level 2. Lie on your stomach. Place your hands on your head. Gently lift your upper torso. Hold for eight counts. Slowly return. Lift just the legs. Hold for eight counts. Slowly return.

Level 3. Repeat the aforementioned, only lift your torso and legs at the same time. Hold for eight counts.

Note: Avoid this exercise if you have any back problems.

Floor Back Attitude

Level 3. In a push up position. Lift your buttocks off the floor as you straighten your arms. Extend one leg up and bend the leg into an attitude position. Arch the back as the lifted leg touches the floor. Hold for eight counts. Return and repeat on other side.

Arm Strength

Push Ups

Level 1. Begin in a prone position. Lift the torso up keeping the knees on the ground, the back flat and the arms straight. Bend the arms and perform eight modified push ups.

Level 2. Perform the above, only with the knees straight and off the floor.

Level 3. Perform sixteen push-ups with a short break after eight.

Level 4. Increase the number of push-up repetitions or do eight push ups with one leg extended.

Triceps Push Up

Level 1. In a sitting position and with your feet parallel, place your hands behind your hips with your fingers pointing towards your buttocks. Lift the hips up and then bend your arms as you lower your body without touching your hips on the floor. Repeat eight times.

Level 2. Repeat the above only increase the number of repetitions to sixteen with a short pause after eight.

Level 3. Repeat the above only lift one leg parallel to the ground. Perform eight repetitions, then repeat with your other leg.

Level 4. Repeat the above only increase the number of repetitions to sixteen with a short pause after eight.

Isolation Exercise Technique

The isolation of your hips, torso, head and shoulders as well as the opposition of these and other body parts, is what makes jazz dance so unique from other forms of dance. Isolation is the separation of a particular part of the body from the whole body for a given movement. The technique used in this exercise section is designed to teach you control of the different anatomical parts of your body used in isolation. For the novice dancer isolation movement can feel unnatural, but continual use of the isolation technique can result in strong discipline and body control. The following exercises should begin with eight counts for each movement and diminish to lesser counts of four, two, and one. Special consideration should be given to the neck. Use caution with any neck exercises to avoid injury. Before performing any neck exercise, place your hand on your head and perform the movements listed below slowly with resistance (pressing your head against your hand) through the full range of motion. Then continue with the exercise.

Head

Level 1. Tilt the head forward, center, back, center, Then forward, back, forward, back. *Note:* Do not extend your head too far backwards. Instead, maintain control by extending your head only to the point of control and comfort.

Level 1. Tilt your head right, center, left, center, then right, left, right, left. *Note:* Keep your shoulders pressed down.

Level 1. Look over your right shoulder, center, left shoulder, center, then right, left, right left. *Note:* Focus on a point with your eyes when turning your head side to side.

Level 1. Roll your head one-half of the way to the right, one-half roll to the left, then all the way around and reverse.

Level 2. Perform all of the above head exercises while walking forward for eight counts and backward for eight counts.

Level 3. Step to the right, touch your left foot next to your right. Repeat with other foot. Add the different head isolations while performing this foot pattern.

Level 3. Egyptian head movements forward and back and side to side. *Note:* Pressing your hands against each other over your head will make the head movement easier.

Caution: Avoid any type of head tilts or rolls if you have neck or back problems.

Shoulders

Level 1. Begin with your arms in second position. Lift your shoulders up, forward, up. Press down into place. Lift your shoulders up, backward, up, and press down again. Repeat alternating shoulders one forward and one backward.

Level 1. Lift your shoulders up, forward, down, and back. Reverse. Roll shoulders back and then forward.

Level 2. Perform all of the above shoulder exercises while walking forward for eight counts and backwards for eight counts.

Level 3. Begin in jazz first position. Step your right leg to jazz second position as your shoulder lifts up and forward. Return and repeat with your other side.

Level 3. Alternate your shoulders forward and back while walking with your arms in an upward fifth position.

Level 3. Alternate shoulder rolls while walking forward and backward.

Level 4. Perform all of the above at a faster tempo. Shimmy shoulders in a 1, 2, 1-2-3 rhythm while traveling.

Arms

Note: Another term used to describe the carriage of your arms is called "port de bras."

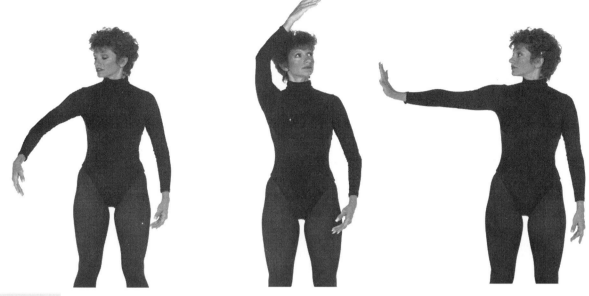

Level 1. Right arm softly comes from a ballet first position to a second position, to a high fifth position, down to your rib cage. "Press" out to the second position with a flexed palm. Return to a low first position. Repeat with your left arm. Repeat with both arms.

Level 1. Bend your arms to your chest with jazz palms for one count. Bring your elbows sharply in for the second count. Straighten sharply to a high fifth position for one count. Sharply drop your arms to second position for one count. Softly port de bras your right arm in an inward circle to second position for two counts. Repeat with left arm.

Finger Isolations

A good idea for individuals who have excess tension in their hands are finger isolations. Try touching each finger with your thumb as you walk, beginning with your little finger and then reversing.

Ribs

| Right | Left | Forward | Back |

Level 1. Place your hands on your shoulders or on your hips. Move your rib cage right, center, left, and then center, taking care not to let your shoulders drop or your hips move. Next move your ribs left, right, left, right. Move your rib cage forward, center, back, and then center, keeping your stomach lifted and your shoulders down. Then move just forward, back, forward, back. (Imagine your ribs are placed on a table and keep them level as they move from side to side.) Move your rib cage forward, right, back, left, then attempt a rib circle motion. Reverse.

Level 2. Do all of the above while walking forward for eight counts and backward for eight counts.

Level 3. Double and triple the rib cage movements in the same amount of time as you did the single movements.

Level 4. Triple the ribs movements while traveling side to side, front, and back.

Level 4. Perform a full arch-contract exercise. Step to jazz second position, as you release your rib cage and head with arms in jazz second position with jazz palms. Place your feet together as you contract your rib cage and lower your head. Your arms come in to our rib cage. Step one foot behind in a forward lunge at the same time releasing your head and ribs with one arm in high fifth and the other arm on your hip. Step your feet together in a contracted position again. Repeat the lunge with your other side. Step your feet together in a contracted position.

Hips

Note: One of the keys to moving your hips freely and easily is to stay in a demi-plié making sure your toes are facing forward. Hip isolations are performed by contracting your inside thigh muscles. Be sure not to move your ribs when isolating!

| Right | Left | Forward | Back |

Level 1. Jazz feet and arms in second position demi-plié. Move your hips right, center, left, center, then right, left, right, left. Next, move your hips forward, center, back, center, then forward, back, forward, back. Rock hips right, left, right, left. Move hips to the right corner of the room, then center, left corner, and center again.

Level 1. Move your hips to all four corners, front, right, back, left, then hip roll to the right very slowly and gradually speed up. Reverse.

Level 2. Try all the above while walking as your arms come from second position to a high fifth position, then back to the second position.

Level 2. Perform double and triple time hip movements in place.

Level 3. Double and triple the hip movements while traveling. Do a walking hip roll.

Level 4. Try all of the above at a faster tempo. Perform a hip roll with a step touch foot pattern. Change foot pattern to step-together-step, then change the pattern to a chaîné turn.

Level 4.   Move the head, arms and ribs at the same time. Begin in jazz second position with your arms and feet. Isolate your head, arms, and ribs at the same time. Your ribs go right as your right arm bends in to your rib cage and your head looks right. Your ribs go center as your right hand extends to second position and your head looks forward. Repeat with your left side. Next, contract your ribs as both your arms come in and your head drops forward. Return to center as your arms go to second. Release your ribs as both of your arms stay in the second position and your head releases back. Reverse the entire combination (left, center, right, center, release, and contract).

Level 4.   Repeat the above with your hips instead of your ribs.

Knees

Level 1.   Perform a side lunge with knee facing in. Turn your knee out again. Repeat with your other side.

Feet

Level 1.   Begin in jazz first position. Tendu your right foot. Flex your ankle, then point your foot. Return to the ball of your foot, then return your foot to first position. Repeat with your other foot. Repeat the tendu only rotate the foot clockwise then counterclockwise. Repeat with your other foot. Repeat the above in a turned out (ballet first) position.

5 Kicks (Battements)

Before a good grand battement (big kick) can be attained, you should be warm and flexible in the muscles and joints associated with that particular kick. Therefore, you must focus on the importance of flexibility (see S-t-r-e-t-c-h-ability chapter). By increasing the flexibility in your legs you will enhance your chances for feelings of accomplishment as well as reduce injuries and strain. Once you have achieved the desired range of motion you should concentrate on both strength and control. This is demonstrated by the various exercises in this chapter.

When kicking, always keep your legs straight unless otherwise specified. Guard against moving at the small of your back by lifting up in your stomach. Refrain from bending or leaning heavily on your support-ing leg. It is very important to establish a center as the source of control and not let your lifted leg pull your hips out of alignment. Watch for tension in your neck and wrists. That is a sign that your center has been lost. Always square your hips and shoulder to the front. Mentally "reach" with your toe if your foot is pointed, or with your heel if your foot is flexed. Let your leg do the lifting. Imagine lifting the front muscles "underneath." Eventually, coming down from a kick should occur because you choose to return to the floor when desired, not because you have to return. To follow these exercise progressions correctly, try getting your leg higher and in more control as the tempo increases. First learn to use your feet correctly by performing the following exercise:

Level 1. From jazz first position, "brush" the floor by pressing against the floor with the ball of your foot until your foot is approximately three inches off the floor. Repeat the brush, each time getting higher and higher for eight repetitions. Repeat with your opposite foot. Repeat in ballet first position. Brush forward leading with your heel, brush to the side, brush back eight times each. Feel how the brushing effect helps lift your leg off the floor.

Grand Battement

Level 1.   Begin in jazz parallel lunge position with your arms in second position. Kick your back leg forward and straighten both legs. Return to lunge. Do four with a pointed toe and four with a flexed foot. Repeat with your other leg.

Level 2.   Repeat the above beginning in ballet fourth position and maintaining a turn out.

Level 1.   In ballet fourth position with your arms in second, kick side keeping your hips down and your knee facing up to the ceiling. Return to the lunge position after each kick. Kick four times with pointed foot and four times with a flexed foot. Spiral turn 180° and repeat with your other leg.

Level 1. In the ballet fourth position with your arms in second, lunge forward. Brush your front foot backward lifting your leg as high as possible. Turn your knee out and make sure your foot is directly behind you, not out to the side. Return to lunge. Kick four times with a pointed toe, then four times with a flexed foot. Repeat with your other leg.

Level 3. All of the above kicks (front, side and back) and relevé on the kick.

Level 4. Grand battement front, side, and back while traveling across the floor. Relevé on each kick.

Plié-Relevé Grand Battement

Level 2.   In jazz first position with your arms in second, kick your right foot front with your supporting left foot in plié-relevé position. Step your right foot back in a lunge. Step your left foot to the second position. Step your right foot forward. Kick your left foot front in plié relevé position. Step your left foot back with your right foot in second position and your left forward. Repeat. This also can be performed with kicks to the side and back.

Level 3.   In the ballet first position with long, low jazz arms, kick with pointed toe to second position, extending your leg outward as you kick, and arch your back. Place foot down and wrap your arms around your body.

Fan Kick

Level 1.   Begin in ballet first position with your arms in second. Perform an outside circle (rond de jambe) by sliding the working foot front and carry your toes in an arc along the ground, then return to first position. Repeat eight times without disturbing the immobility of your torso. After performing on the other leg, try lifting the leg off the ground keeping your knees turned out. To build strength, perform a single fan kick, alternating each leg four times with a plié at the beginning of the lift.

Level 2.   In ballet second position with your arms in second, brush your leg in an outward circle from your hip with a straight leg and end by lunging to the back. Perform an inward fan kick rotation by rotating your straight leg inward and ending in a side lunge. Make sure your knee is in a turned out position in all rotations. The rotation is done in front of your body and your supporting leg is either straight or in a plié-relevé position. Repeat with your other leg.

Level 3.   Perform the aforementioned only increase the height of the kick.

Attitude Swings

Level 1.   Begin the ballet first position with the second position jazz arms. Tendu side with your right foot. Swing your right leg across your body into an attitude front. Return swing across your body to an attitude side. Swing your right leg again across your body and continue a complete inward rotation. Reverse by swinging your leg outward, then inward. Rotate your leg outward ending in an attitude side. Place your foot in the ballet first position. Repeat with your other side.

Level 2.   Same as above, but every time your leg swings across your body, demi-plié to create an up and down rhythm.

Level 3.   Same as above, but every time your leg swings across your body relevé on the supporting leg.

Hinge Kick

Level 1 and 2. See Strength Technique Exercises of Warm Up Chapter.

Level 3. In a hinge position, développé one leg out into a grand battement with supporting leg in plié-relevé position.

Layout Side Kick

Level 3. Grand battement in second position (to the side). Arch your body at the highest point of the kick and "follow through" with your leg as it returns to the floor.

Layover to a Kick

Level 4.   Perform a tabletop layover. Rotate your body 90° towards your extended leg, then arch the body as you grand battement.

Hitchkick

Level 2. Begin with a small forward lunge with your left foot front and turned out. Kick your right leg up and switch your left leg forward in flight. Land on your right leg first. Repeat with your other leg. This can be done to the front, side, or back.

Level 3. Begin with a jazz jump instead of a lunge (as illustrated).

Level 4. Hitchkick layout. As you put your second leg down, "layout" the body by arching your back and swinging the arms through to high fifth position.

Illusion

Level 4.   Swing one leg into an arabesque. Do not stop at the arabesque. Instead continue the leg through to make a complete circle while the chest drops to the knee and returns to original position.

The dos and do nots of a grand battement include:

Do

- Work on flexibility in your legs.
- Use your feet as an aid to lift your leg by "brushing" the floor.
- Square your hips.
- Imagine lifting your leg from underneath.
- Lift your rib cage up while keeping your shoulders down and your body in alignment.
- Keep your legs straight unless otherwise indicated.
- Breathe naturally to avoid tension.
- Point your toes unless otherwise indicated.

Do Not

- Lose control of your arms.
- Bend your supporting leg unless otherwise indicated.
- Drop your chest.
- Place unnecessary weight on your supporting hip.
- Look down.
- Get tense.

6 Turns, Turns, Turns

Turns are one of the most exciting elements of dance. And they are not that hard! Remember the acronym "CASTS" the next time you perform a successful turn. This is a key to turning whether you are attempting a beginning turn or six successive advanced turns.

C = Center

A = Arms

S = Spotting

T = Timing

S = Strength

As explained earlier in this book, one cannot stress enough the importance of a good *center* (See Warm-Up Chapter). If your body falls out of alignment even slightly when you are turning, the momentum of the turning "force" will throw you off balance. Practice working on your center by "pressing" into the ground when you relevé on one foot, then holding your balance in the relevé position as long as possible.

The second key to turning is *arm control*. Arms vary in jazz dance (depending on the type of turn), but there is a standard arm position used if you are a beginner. It is called an "open-close-open" position. "Open" refers to the second position jazz or ballet arms and "close" refers to the ballet fifth en avant position arms. By closing to the fifth position in the middle of a turn you are shortening your radius, thus gaining more momentum and speed. Try closing your eyes and *feeling* the "open-close-open" position as you go through the motions. Controlling your arms can assist you in a turn. Flyaway arms can throw you from your center, thus causing you to fall forward, backwards, or even to the side. Keep your elbows lifted, and retain strength in your upper back when turning. The feeling should be almost as though you were pressing your arms downward against an imaginary table or hugging a large beach ball. Keep your shoulders down to avoid losing your center. The force and speed of opening and closing your arms will assist you in multiple turns.

Spotting is the process enabling the execution of a number of turns without getting dizzy. It also helps you find your balance and center, and can assist you in starting and stopping your rotation. A good way to learn spotting is to focus your eyes forward (without lifting or dropping the chin) at a natural level and at a specific object—real or imagined—on a wall or in space. Begin rotating your body in a circle, keeping your eyes focused on the object. When you have reached the point where your body is turned as far as it can with your head still unmoved, quickly turn your head around, in a complete rotation as quickly as possible, letting your body follow. In other words, in a turn, your head is the last part of your body to leave and the first to return. Gradually increase the speed of turning and continue doing as many repetitions as you can. Then try the opposite direction.

Timing is developed through consistent practice. At the start of your turn, think of lifting up to relevé before you pull in the arms to execute a turn, and remember to spot. The timing will feel different when you perform two, three, or four turns on one leg. Your speed will be greater as you increase the number of turns. You will need to find your own timing. Try practicing to different tempos and beats. Remember, practicing everyday with correct technique will guarantee results!

Here is where *strength* is truly tested. The arms need to have the strength to assist in balance and force. Abdominal and back strength are needed to control your center and your calf muscles must be strong enough to hold you in relevé on one leg while you perform multiple turns. Practice heel raises with one foot while holding onto a ballet barre or chair for balance. Do three sets of ten repetitions with about sixty seconds in between. Practice this every other day, then hold the relevé position for ten seconds while you visually imagine yourself performing ten turns. Yes! That's right, ten turns! Visualization is the first step to performing a goal.

Two-Footed Turns

Pivot Turn

Level 1. Begin in jazz first position. Step with your right foot front and lift your left heel, staying in plié. Pivot 180° to the left. Step on the left foot and bring your right foot to the front again and repeat. Reverse with your other side. *Note:* Lead with your hip and roll off your back foot when stepping to the front, and spot front.

1   2   3

4

Three Step Turn

Level 1. Step right to right for the first count with your arms in second position. Turn your body 180° to the right as you step left on count two. Continue turning your body another 180° to the right. Then step right on count three. Touch your left foot next to the right to complete the rotation on count four. Your knees are slightly bent and you are stepping on the whole of the foot. Your head spots to the right. Repeat. Reverse with your other side.

Level 1. Variation: On count four when your left foot touches, contract your pelvis and accent the contraction with your right arm by giving it a sword-like effect motion inward to your rib cage.

Level 2. Substitute a "ball change" (see Locomotor Chapter) for the last touch movement.

Chainé Turn

Level 1. Similar to the three step turn only keep your momentum going into a series of turns in one direction. Keep your arms closed to the fifth position while turning and open to the second position after completion of a turn. Your head spots either forward or to the side. Your legs are straight and always relevé. *Note:* Every turn is approximately one foot in width apart.

Level 1. Variation: Touch your hand lightly on your shoulders while turning. This exercise is good for practicing foot movement and spotting.

Level 1. Variation: On count four (when your left foot touches), contract your pelvis and accent the contraction with your right arm by giving it a sword-like effect motion inward towards your rib cage.

Level 2. Variation: Substitute a ball change for the last touch movement.

Level 2. Variation: A good exercise is to do four consecutive turns high, four low, four high, etc. Always turn on the ball of the foot and keep your arms in fifth during the entire series.

Level 2. Variation: On each continuous chainé turn, change arm positions from first, to second, to a high fifth position.

Level 2. Perform low chainés in a plié-relevé position.

Paddle Turn

Level 1.   Switch from the ball of one foot to the ball of the other as you turn in a circle, creating a soft up and down rhythm. Your body is bent at a slight angle toward the direction of the turn. Lead with your shoulders and arms in a "wrap" position around your body, but slightly away from your body, with your front arm in the ballet low fifth position.

Pencil Turn

Level 1.   Begin in a side lunge position with your arms in the second position. Bring your feet together by placing your extended leg tightly next to your bent leg. With your legs straight, close your arms to the fifth position and rotate 360° outside (backwards). Squeeze your legs together while spotting to the front. This turn is done with your weight on the balls of both feet. End the rotation by bringing your arms out to the second position again.

Soutenu Turn

Level 2. From ballet second position, draw your right foot straight into the ballet fifth position and relevé to the front (you can also go to the back). Turn left 360° on both feet and end with your left foot in front. Your arms come from second position, to a high fifth position, to second again.

Spiral Turn

Level 2. In a demi-plié, cross one foot in front of the other. Keeping your feet in place, rotate 360°. Notice that your legs will end up in a switched position.

Hip Roll Turn

Level 2.   In a demi-plié, cross your right leg behind your left leg at the same time bring your pelvis forward. Keep your feet in place and rotate 360° to the right while your hips make a complete circle to the right, back, left, and front. Two hip rolls can be done in one turn.

Level 3.   Variation: Grand plié during the first half of the turn, then spiral up during the last half.

Drag Turn

Level 2.   Step left to your left side in a small lunge turned out, with your arms in third position. Pivot to the left on your left foot and turn 360° while dragging your right foot next to your left on the side of your big right toe.

Outside Pas de Bourrée Turn

Level 2.   This is a three-step turn performed with the first two steps on the ball of the foot and the last step with the entire foot in a plié-relevé position. Begin with your feet and arms in jazz second position. Step left to left turning your body 120° to the left. Continue turning 120° to the left and step on your right. Complete the 360° turn by crossing your left foot in front of your right. The spot occurs on the second step.

Chaîné Fan Kick Turn

Level 3.   Perform a low chaîné turn to the left (step left, right). Instead of placing your left foot for the third step, lift your foot into an outward fan kick rotation. Place your left foot down after the fan kick. Turn 180° to your left and step right. Fan your left foot again as you turn 180°. Repeat continuously.

Level 4.   Perform the above, but layout the fan kick before placing it on the ground.

One Footed Turns

Barrel Turn

Level 2.   Similar to a pencil turn, only your body is bent forward from your trunk with eye contact toward the audience. Your arms are in jazz second position, creating a windmill effect.

Low Jazz Walk Turn

Level 1.   Step with your right foot forward in a low jazz walk position (see Locomotive Chapter). Pivot 360° to the outside left, with your knee in the forward passé position and your supporting leg in a plié-relevé position. Step left foot down. Walk right and repeat keeping your spot to the front. Reverse.

Outside Jazz Pirouette

Level 1. Begin in jazz fourth position with your front foot flat and your back heel lifted with your weight balanced between the two legs and your arms in ballet third position. Bring your left foot to a forward passé position. Relevé on your supporting leg as you close your arms to a low fifth position. Hold for two counts. Step down on your left foot and extend your right leg to the side with your toes pointed and your arms in the second position. Repeat with your other side. Count as follows:

1   ➜   Place your left foot in jazz fourth position

2   ➜   Plié

3–4   ➜   Passé left and relevé your right foot

5   ➜   Step down on left foot

6   ➜   Point right foot to right side

7–8   ➜   Hold, then repeat with your other side.

Level 1.   Repeat the same as above only instead of holding for two counts, perform a full turn on your right leg to the outside (to the left). Repeat on your other side.

Level 2.   Two full jazz turns instead of one in the same amount of time on relevé.

Level 1.   Low outside pirouette. Perform the pirouette in a plié-relevé position instead of a relevé position.

Level 2.   Perform two full jazz turns in plié-relevé.

Level 3.   Three turns in a relevé position.

Level 3.   Three turns in a plié-relevé position.

Level 4.   Four or more turns in a relevé position.

Level 4.   Four or more turns in a plié-relevé position.

Note: If you are performing a single turn and your arm preparation is in the third position, you only need to close your arms from the third position to the fifth position to give yourself the momentum of one turn. At the end of your turn, the opening of your arms to second position assists in stopping you. For two or more turns, prepare your arms in the third position, but open your front arm to second position before closing in the fifth position. For example, in the outside jazz pirouette, quickly open your left arm to the second position, then close to the fifth position as you begin turning. You will get more momentum for the number of turns you need. For more than three turns, repeat the above only gradually bring your arms closer to your body while you turn in order to shorten your radius.

Inside Jazz Pirouette

Level 1.   Begin in a side lunge with your right knee bent. Step in relevé onto a straight left leg and turn to the left (inside). Come down on your right leg and end in a left lunge. Repeat with your other side.

Level 2.   Two inside pirouettes at the same tempo.

Level 3.   Three inside pirouettes.

Level 4.   Four or more inside pirouettes.

Low Inside Jazz Pirouette

All of the above are performed in a plié-relevé position.

Ballet Pirouette

Level 1. Begin in ballet fifth position with your right foot back. Tendu your left foot to the left and continue the foot to the back in ballet fourth demi-plié position. With your arms in third position, close to the fifth position as you relevé on your right foot while your left foot goes to a turned out passé position. Turn left (outside). End in ballet fifth position with your left foot front and arms in second position. Repeat with your other side.

Level 2. Perform the above ballet pirouette, only turn right (inside) which means your arms will have to change in the third position with your right arm forward and your left arm in the second position. Repeat with your other side.

Level 2. Perform double inside and outside ballet pirouettes.

Level 2. Perform pirouettes from ballet second position and ballet fifth position instead of fourth position.

Level 3. Perform an inside pirouette and kick out to a second position after rotating 360°. End in ballet fifth position. Repeat with your other side.

Level 3. Perform an outside pirouette and extend leg into a back arabesque after rotating 360° or more. Repeat with your other side.

Arabesque Turn

Level 2.   Begin in ballet fourth position with your left foot forward. Turn 360° outward (to the left) on your left supporting foot with your right leg extended backward in a back arabesque. Arm position is optional. Repeat with your other side.

Level 2.   Same as an the arabesque turn above only the back leg is in an attitude position.

Attitude Turn

Level 3.   Begin in ballet fourth position with your left foot forward. Left arm swings in front of the body as your right arm goes behind. Ron de jambe your left leg to an attitude position, then continue the force of the leg around in an outside 360° rotation. Arms vary. End in ballet fifth with left foot front.

Piqué Turn

Level 2.   Begin with your body facing the right in ballet fifth position with your left foot front and arms in ballet third position. Point our left foot to the left and quickly step on it with a straight leg in relevé. At the same time bring your right foot to a turned out passé position with toes of the right foot slightly in front of the left knee. Close arms to fifth position as you turn 360° on the supporting leg to the inside (left). Come down on your right leg in demi-plié with your left foot extended to the side and slightly lifted off the floor with your arms in second position Repeat in a series. Repeat on your other side.

Level 3.   Perform a single, single, then double piqué series with fluidity.

Pike Turn

Level 3.   This turn is performed in the same manner as a ballet outside pirouette from fourth position, only the non-supporting leg is in a pike position instead of a passé position.

Fouetté Turn

Level 4.   This turn is a series of turns on your supporting leg, whipping your working leg in a quarter circle while turning. Begin in ballet fifth position with your left foot front. Tendu left, then ballet fourth position with left foot back. Execute an outside single pirouette with your left foot in a sur le cou-de-pied position (a low passé position with the left foot wrapped around the right ankle). Then thrust your working leg energetically forward at a 45° angle across the right leg at the same time demi-plié the supporting right leg. Swing your working leg to second position in the air while rising and turning one the relevé of your right foot. Whip your working leg inward passing your toe quickly from the back to the front of your supporting knee. To continue a series, thrust your working leg forward and descend easily on each turn by a demi-plié on your supporting leg. Open your arms to second position at the termination of each turn.

Combination Turns

Level 3.

1. Chainé to pencil turn series.

2. Chassé, barrel turn, chassé, barrel turn jump.

3. Series of piqué turns in a circle.

4. Outside pas de bouree turn. Use the last step as a preparation and pirouette outside on your supporting leg. Step forward left, right and reverse.

5. Tendu second position, then to ballet fourth position into an outside pirouette, bring working foot down to ballet fifth and jump into a second position and pirouette again.

Level 4.

1. Triple pirouette immediately in a jump.

2. Outside double pirouette into an attitude position.

3. Chassé into a barrel turn to a stag jump then pivot soutenu turn to a layout.

4. Chainé, chainé, double tour l'air.

5. Walk four steps to ballet fourth position, single pike turn, pull knee into a double pirouette while performing a head roll.

6. Kick ball change into and outside double jazz pirouette. Step down on your working foot and perform an inside jazz piouette. Step down on your working foot and ball change into an outside pirouette immediately into a back arabesque turn.

7 Locomotive Movements

Locomotive movements, or total body motion, require quick weight shifting and concentrated centering. It is recommended that you initially concentrate on obtaining an overview of the total locomotive section before trying to learn the individual techniques.

As you practice learning these steps and movements, learn them in this order, 1) Concentrate on successfully completing your foot movements first. 2) Concentrate on learning the arm motions along with the foot movements. 3) Work on adding your other body parts such as your hips. Do no try to learn everything at once. Always maintain good posture (center) and eye contact. Never look down. Instead, look directly where you are going.

Make sure you have the proper techniques before progressing. Not only will these techniques give you the strength and consistency you will need for dancing, but they will enable you to dance longer by reducing your chance of being injured.

Practice with enough space to cover at least twenty-four counts of walks. Remember, technique becomes exciting when you give it meaning and expression.

WALKS

Level 1. The first most important step is to be able to walk to the count of the music beat. Begin by just walking across the floor stepping with the beat of the music. Step on every beat and count to yourself by counts of eight (1,2,3,4,5,6,7,8,1,2,...). Now try "half counting" (stepping on every two counts) to the music. Let's go faster and "double time" by stepping two times to a single beat while you count out loud (1&2&3&4&5...). As you advance you will be able to go from one rhythm to another without stopping. When traveling across the floor in a class situation it is almost standard that you wait for the person to go in front of you for eight counts before you begin.

As you walk naturally your arms should swing in opposition. Most walks and traveling steps are performed in opposition unless otherwise specified by the choreographer. For arm control and awareness keep your arms down to your side and slightly behind your hips. Remember to keep your chest and stomach lifted and your eye contact forward.

Toe-Ball-Heel Walk

Perform a toe-ball-heel action with your feet as you walk across the floor to the beat of the music.

Relevé Walk

Keeping your legs straight (do not lock the knees), and on relevé, walk across the floor. This walk strengthens the calf muscles and assists you in "feeling" the leg position for chaine turns.

Hip Walk

Leading with your knee and hip, walk forward with slightly bent knees, keeping your toes forward (your knees should almost touch when passing each other).

Back Hip Walk

Your hips push to the back as you step forward in a demi-plié. Keep your toes forward and your trunk slightly forward. Optional arms are wiggling your fingers in jazz hand positions.

Low Jazz Walk

Demi-plié your toes forward. Roll from your heel to the ball of your foot as you step forward. Keep your palms open, your arms in opposition, and your trunk upright. Be sure to keep low and level.

Toe Drag Walk

Step forward in a demi-plié. Drag your back foot, keeping your leg straight, and sliding on the side of your big toe. Your shoulders should alternate slightly. Repeat with your other leg.

Character Walk

Facing to the side with your elbows in and jazz hands out. Look over your slightly lifted shoulder. Leading with your rib cage, lean back and walk to the side crossing one foot over the other every other step.

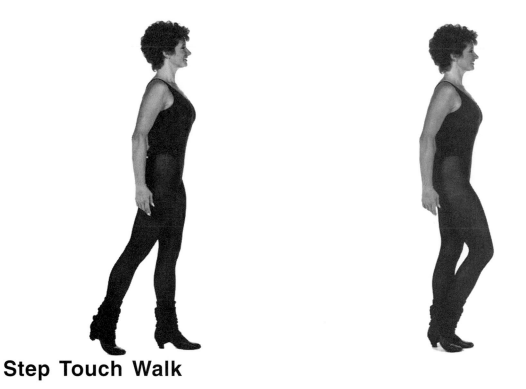

Step Touch Walk

Step forward on your right foot, bringing your left foot to your right and touching your foot beside it. Repeat with your other leg.

Cross Touch Walk

Demi-plié with your feet parallel, crossing your right foot over your left foot. Touch your left foot to the side with a fully extended leg and a pointed leg and pointed toe. Repeat to the other side.

LA Walk

Facing to your left, lift your working hip up and bring your foot and hip down in a toe-ball-heel action. Cross over with your other foot. Keep your arms down at your sides behind your hips.

Vegas Walk

Lift your knee to the passé inward position, crossing your other foot on relevé while keeping your legs straight. Step on the lifted foot and repeat with your other side.

Attitude Twist Walk

Step right in a demi-plié. At the same time lift your left leg in a back attitude and twist to the right as far as possible. Step your left leg forward in a demi-plié and an attitude right. Repeat.

Mirror Walk

Partners begin facing each other. As they walk sideways in unison in a step behind step pattern, one partner copies the others arm movements with one leading and one following. Mirror each others arms as the arms come from the first position to second to high fifth then back to first position.

Camel Walk

Step forward on your right heel. Roll to the ball of your foot, at the same time you roll your hips forward. Finish with your left foot coming to the right. Repeat.

Walking Combinations

Level 2, 3 and 4. Combine different walks together. For example, perform two of each type of walk as you travel across the floor. Change direction by walking backwards or sideways. Speed up the tempo.

Traveling Steps

Ball Change

Level 1. Transfer your weight from one foot to another with the ball of your foot, then the entire foot. This can be done in any direction.

Cross Ball Change

Level 1. Step right over left. Switch from the ball of your left foot to the ball of your right foot. This should be performed in the following manner: full foot, ball, full foot. Repeat with your other side.

Level 2. Perform a cross ball change changing directions by crossing your right foot over left foot while you turn one quarter to the right and ball change. Reverse.

Kick Ball Change

Level 1. Small kick with your right foot. Ball change right, left.

Level 2. Perform a traveling kick ball change by executing a small kick with the right foot (similar to "flicking" the foot). Place the ball of your right foot where your supporting left foot is. Walk left forward. Repeat continuously.

Chassé (shah say) Jazz

Level 1. Step, together, step, in a "1 and 2" rhythm, performed in a plié-relevé position leading with your hips. Performed ball, ball, flat, to the corners of the room.

Chassé Ballet

Level 1.   From the ballet fifth position, place your foot forward and slide your right leg forward in demi-plié. From this position, push both your legs up from the floor to meet in the air in a tightly pressed fifth position. To finish, your back leg should land in a plié while your right leg immediately slides forward in a demi-plié ready to spring up again.

Level 2.   Perform a jazz chassé with a one-half turn. Chassé right facing your left side. Pick up your left foot, one-half turn to the left (outside) and chassé left.

Chugs

Level 1.   Traveling in the air while hopping on one foot.

Grapevine

Level 1.　Facing to the side, step your right foot to your right side. Your left foot crosses behind your right foot. Step your right foot to your right side. Your left foot crosses in front of your right foot. Keep repeating.

Level 2.　Grapevine with a rhythm change. Facing left and continually traveling, step right on the count of "1," cross left on "2," step right cross left on "and 3," step right cross left on "and 4."

Passé Lunge Backwards

Level 1.　Walk backwards lifting your leg in the passé position, turning in before stepping. After eight counts repeat with your knee in passé turned out.

Jazz Square

Level 1. Steps are taken in a square pattern. Your right foot steps across in front of your left foot. Step back on your left foot. Step to the right side on your right foot. Step forward on your left foot. This can be done with either foot leading.

Jazz Shoot

Level 1. The footwork is almost the same as the jazz square, but there is an additional chug. On your right foot step across in front of your left foot. Chug back on your right foot. Step back on your left foot. Step to the right on your right foot, and step forward on your left foot.

1 2 3

4 5

Lindy

Level 1. Also known as a chassé ball change. Step, together, step (right, left, right) to the right, step back on the ball of your left foot. Step forward on your right foot. Repeat with your other side.

Side Slide

Level 1.   Facing your left side, cross your left over right in a demi-plié. Large lunge to the right by pushing hard with your left foot. At the same time slide your left foot towards your right foot until it crosses over your right foot again. This slide can be done backwards by lifting your leg into a back scale with a force that will make your supporting foot slide backward on the ground.

Suzy Q

Level 1. Standing in the first position parallel, turn your toes to the right. Still moving to the right, turn both heels to the right, then your toes again, heels, toes. Continue to repeat.

Sugar Foot

Level 1. Step on the ball of your right foot with your knee turned out, then pivot on your right foot so that your right knee turns in. Step forward to the left with your knee turned out. Pivot with your knee rotating inward. The pivot and the next step may be done simultaneously. Switch hips as you travel, and wiggle your hands for style.

Jazz Run

Level 1. Staying low to the ground, perform large lunges while running and sliding your back leg on the side of your large toe. Turn your feet out. Place your arms in opposition of your feet. When the run is perfected try alternating your shoulders.

Grand Battements Traveling Forward

Level 1. Front kick with your right, then your left and side kick with your right, then your left. Walk four steps in between.

Level 2. Développé front kick with your right, then your left in a turned out position. Walk four steps and repeat kicking to the side.

Level 3. Perform the aforementioned only relevé when performing the kick.

Traveling Balances

Level 1. Step four walks forward and balance in a low arabesque for two counts. Repeat with other leg.

Level 2. Step four walks and balance in arabesque for four counts in turned out position. Variation: Repeat above, but perform a back attitude instead of an arabesque. Repeat again, but perform a front attitude instead of an arabesque.

Level 3. Perform the aforementioned only perform the balance positions on relevé.

Pas de Bourrée
(pah deh boo ray)

Level 2.   These three steps can be performed in many directions. Begin in the plié-relevé position. Cross your left foot behind your right. Step with your right foot to the right side. Step with your left foot to the front (ball, ball, flat). This can be done in a single or a half-count rhythm, but should not be confused with a step ball change as the rhythm is different.

Level 2.   Variation: Pas de bourrée traveling backwards. Performed same as above only step backward instead of forward on the third step.

Level 2.   Variation: Pas de bourrée traveling sideways. When performing this step continuously, you will need to begin facing the side and step in second position in between each pas de bourrée. The third step goes to the side instead of to the front or back.

Level 2.   Outside pas de bourrée turn. See Turns, Turns, Turns Chapter.

Combination Traveling Steps

The following traveling steps are self-explanatory. At the advanced levels, the transitions from one skill to another needs to be as fluid as possible and the pattern repeated until you reach the other end of the room. Try speeding up the tempo once the steps are mastered.

Level 2.

1. Chassé side, pas de bourrée side.

2. Chassé side, pas de bourrée side, pivot turn.

Level 3.

1. Four walks front, pas de bourrée, half turning pas de bourrée, half turning pas de bourrée.

2. Alternating single chaine turns with a waltz time ("1-2-3").

3. Chassé side, pas de bourrée side, pivot turn, ball change, pivot turn.

4. Touch lunge, pas de bourrée side, kick ball change, chaine turn.

5. Touch lunge, pas de bourrée side, chaine, kick to a squat position.

6. Walk front two steps, cross grande battement, cross other foot, grande battement other leg, lunge, double out-side pirouette.

7. Walk two steps, chassé, turning pas de bourrée, passé, step second position. Repeat substituting a jazz jump for the passé.

8. Turning pas de bourrée, kick ball change, outside pirouette.

9. Pas de bourrée, jazz jump, pas de bourrée, pirouette.

10. Kick ball change, turning pas de bourrée, outside pirouette, step to fourth position, inside pirouette.

11. Chassé, pas de bourrée, outside pirouette, chaine.

Level 4.

1. Chassé, pivot turn, pas de bourrée, one-half turning pas de bourrée.

2. Pas de bourrée, pas de bourrée, outside pirouette, end facing back. Repeat sequence and end facing front.

3. Side pas de bourrée, jazz jump, step to second position, inside pirouette.

4. Walk layout kick, turning pas de bourrée, outside triple pirouette.

Note: Any of the level two and three combinations can be performed by speeding up the tempo and adding arm variations for a more advanced work out.

Leaps and Jumps

Leaps and jumps make a routine exciting and create a wonderful energy. A jump takes off with two feet and a leap takes off with one foot. Here are some pointers before you get started for safety and good technique: All jumps, hops and leaps should start and land in a demi-plié, coming down on the ball of your foot and then onto your heel. Your rib cage is forward on the leaps and your eye contact should never be down. "Press" into the ground with your foot before taking off. This will create more force and give you additional height. By lifting with your arms (not your shoulders), your arms can assist you in achieving greater height. Arm positions vary depending with the choreographer.

In order to prepare for jumps your feet and legs must be warmed up properly. Do the following exercises for technique and strength no matter what your level is:

Tendu Exercise. In a jazz first position, point your foot forward with the ball of your foot, then your toes. Return to first position. Repeat eight times on each side. Do the same from a ballet first position, first pointing front leading with the heel, then to the side (second position).

Foot Exercise. In jazz first position, lift your foot off the floor by lifting your heel first, then your ball, then your toes. Bring your thigh up by using your muscles in the foot as much as you can. Return your foot to the floor with a toe-ball-heel return. Repeat on each leg ten times. Then prance in place.

Small Jump Exercise. Begin in jazz first position. Take eight small jumps in place making sure you keep your "center" and land in demi-plié after each jump. Eight small jumps from ballet first, second, and fifth position, reversing your feet in the fifth position after each jump.

Tuck Exercise Jumps. Begin in jazz first position. Perform eight tuck jumps, keeping your chest lifted and bringing your knees to your chest.

Straddle Exercise Jumps. Begin with eight straddle jumps from jazz first position, starting low and gradually getting wider and wider.

Arm Exercise. Practice lifting your arms with higher jumps in place. Notice that your arms are the highest when your jump is the highest. Keep your shoulders down to assist you with a good center.

Kick Exercise. Place your hands against a wall (or ballet barre) for support and practice kicking each leg forward eight times quickly. Repeat kicking side and back. (The back kicks are extremely helpful in executing grand jetés.)

Standing Split Exercise. Stand in ballet first position. Jump up and practice splitting the legs (eight on each side) and returning back to first position. Your arms should be in second position at the top of the split.

Level 1

STRAIGHT JUMP   JAZZ JUMP   ARCHED JUMP

JETÉ   CATLEAP

Level 2

TUCK JUMP   ARABESQUE   ATTITUDE JUMP

DOUBLE STAG JUMP   TOUR EN L'AIR   RIGHT ANGLE JUMP

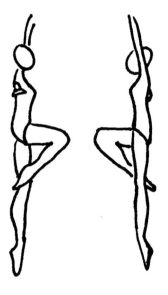

JAZZ JUMP TURN

CONTINUOUS JETÉS

JETÉ IN SECOND POSITION

BACK SLIDE STAG JUMP

Level 3

PIKE JUMP   TUCK JUMP WITH 360° TURN   CABRIOLE

TOE TOUCH

BACK STAG LEAP

BARREL TURN JUMP

FOUETTÉ

TOURJETÉ

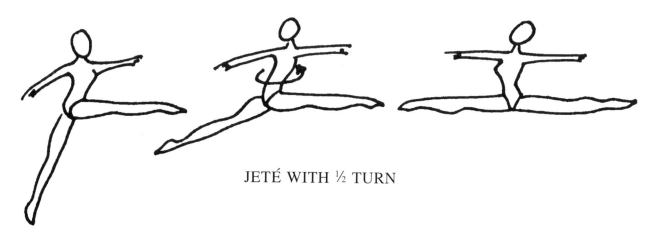

JETÉ WITH ½ TURN

STAG LEAP WITH ½ TURN

AXLE

CHAINÉ JETÉ

Level 4

SPLIT SPLIT JETÉ

DÉVELOPPÉ TO SECOND POSITION

RIGHT ANGLE JUMP WITH 360° TURN

Some combination
jumps include:
CHAINÉ FOUETTÉ AXLE
SINGLE INTO DOUBLE TOUR
CHAINÉ DOUBLE STAG

Floorwork

Floorwork is becoming more and more popular in jazz. It consists of everything from small falls to gymnastics and it adds dynamics and variation to jazz routines. A word of safety: it is a good idea to wear knee pads when trying the moves listed here. It is also recommended that you are a Level 2 dancer before attempting these skills because a certain amount of conditioning and timing is required. Go at your own pace. Because of a lack of space, gymnastics cannot be adequately treated in this book since the skills must be learned in proper technical progression for safety reasons. There are many good gymnastics books on the market today. Following, however is a list of gymnastics skills prominent in jazz dance.

When performing falls, try to carry them out smoothly and quietly. Avoid landing on your knees, elbows, the coccyx or the tip of your shoulders. You can lessen the impact by bending your elbows and cushioning the force with your hands.

Knee Fall

Level 2. Begin in a kneeling position with your arms extended forward and your palms flexed. Fall forward with a straight back, giving at your elbows to cushion the fall.

Front Fall

Level 2.   From a jazz second position, bend slightly forward from the trunk with your arms extended forward and your palms flexed. Fall forward with a straight back and land in a push-up type position, bending at your elbows. Make sure that you control your chest when lowering yourself to the floor.

Back Fall

Level 2.   Contract forward and drop your chin as you bring one foot back. Lower your trunk until your hands touch the floor, then sit back on your posterior and straighten your body out to a supine position on the floor.

Swedish Fall

Level 2. Same as aforementioned only with one leg extended back into an arabesque as you are falling. This is also done with a slight body arch to ease the fall. Your chest touches the floor first.

Side Roll with Straddle (Shoulder Roll)

Level 2.   The shoulder roll should be learned to both sides. For a roll to the left, start in a jazz second position with the feet and the arms. Plié with the left knee and swing the left arm down toward the floor until the forearm and elbow touch the mat momentarily. Then roll onto the left shoulder. Continue rolling with the legs in a straddle position. Roll up onto the bent knee and then step on the left foot.

Knee Roll

Level 2. Begin on your knees with your right leg up. Turn to left 360°. Bring your knees together and lift your left knee up at the end of the turn. The position of your arms is optional, but your arms can help the rotation when you begin in the second position. Then close to fifth position during the turn, and finally return to a second position to help stop the turn.

Knee Slide

Level 2.   Slide onto the knees keeping hips lifted to avoid injury to the knee. Lifting arms assists in slide.

Jazz Split Roll Up

Level 3. Run forward right, left, right. Slide onto the ground with your left leg forward balancing your weight on the left side of your foot. Lift your hips up and travel on your side as much as possible. Your right leg is bent in the jazz split position. During the slide your left hand reaches for the ground, and "pushes" away when it touches the ground giving you more momentum. After sliding, roll onto your stomach, then return to a supine position with your knees bent and your feet slightly apart. Perform a body roll up to a standing position.

Split-Split Series

Level 4.   Begin in a right split position with your arms in the second position. Squeeze your legs together and bring your arms up to a high fifth while lifting your body up and around 180° to a split left position. *Note:* Do not attempt this unless you have a good second position split.

Level 2.

Forward Roll

Back Shoulder Roll

Seat Spin

Swastika Seat Spin

Backbend

Headstand

Handstand

Cartwheel

Level 3.

Walkover

Back Walkover

Tinsica

Running Cartwheel

Cartwheel Succession

Round-Off

Level 4.

Handspring

Back Handspring

Back Flip

Front Flip

Aerial Cartwheel

Aerial Walkover

8 PUTTING IT ALL TOGETHER– CHOREOGRAPHY

To choreograph is to create, and all of us have unlimited creative potential. There's no need to rely on others for choreographic material, you can develop your own. Just as your muscles need time to develop and grow through constant effort, so does the creative consciousness of your mind. How do you begin?

You have by now been exposed to the basic steps and techniques in jazz dance. As a novice, try combining the moves you have just learned. Take a few of the steps and put them together to music you enjoy (for example, a chassé, chaîné turn, jazz square, pas de bourrée), add some trendy moves, your unlimited imagination, a little of your own style, and pow! . . . there's your choreography. For fun, try the steps in reverse (pas de bourrée, jazz square, chaîné turn, chassé). If you are choreographing a class combination, keep the beginning routines short and simple

so you can work on weight transitions, body directions, and smoothness. For the advanced routines you may want to lengthen the routine, add more difficult movements, and change the rhythm so you are not always on the beat of the music.

Choreographing a dance for a professional level class, a production, or a show is a little more difficult. A few pointers that may help you get started include:

1. **Develop a Theme.** This is one of the easiest tasks of choreography. Some examples are: telling a story or idea, a tribute to a musician or a motion picture, centering on a word such as "magic" or "hoe down," or a tribute to a culture. You may prefer just to dance a jazz style to the desired music—lyrical, musical theater, funk, or swing just to name a few. You may want to choose emotions,

117

ideas, images, or an atmosphere as your theme. Perhaps the music you select will give you a story or theme. Make sure the theme fits the age group and audience viewing your performance. To enhance the choreography, take advantage of props, screens, lighting effects, and even live musicians.

2. **Find Your Music.** Music is a great motivating factor for the audience as well as the dancers! Keep the music consistent with your idea or theme. Try diversifying the style of the music or "age" of the music. You can select music from almost all fields: rock, blues, dixieland, soul, country, African, Latin, jazzed up folk, rap, classics, and many more. Just make sure the routine fits the music. Variations can include sounds, poems, words, or even silence. Remember, you can always make the music exciting with your movements.

Analyze the structure of the music. For beginners, develop a chorus where movements can be repeated and irregularities accented. Distinguish which parts of the music will be for individuals and which will be for groups. Note the changes in times, tempos, beats, phrases and energy. Try composing your own music or use live music. One instrument can make an enormous effect. For example, a rhythm matrix can produce variable syncopation to fit your needs. Mixing various songs together in a medley is fun. Get a professional recording studio to assist you, and always try to purchase the best sources of your music to avoid distracting sounds (distortion, etc...). Remember, sometimes music that sounds "OK" in the studio may not be the best quality amplified in a theater or gym.

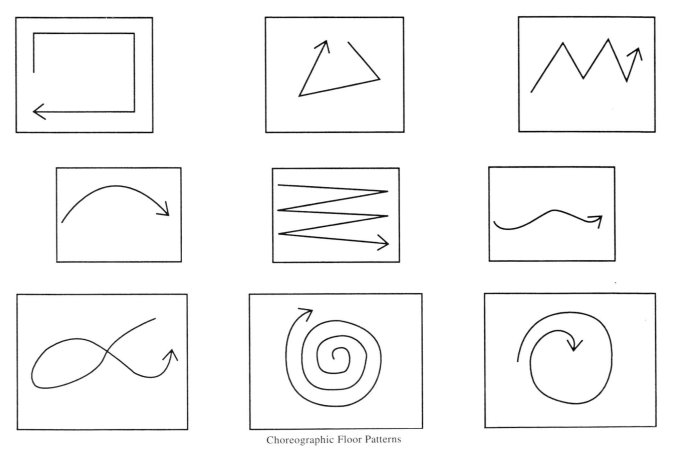

Choreographic Floor Patterns

Choreographic Floor Patterns

3. Developing the Movements. Use the steps and movements in this book as a base for your choreography. Use the entire floor—all the space you have to work with—and be aware of diversity of floor patterns. Be careful of stage designs. For example, symmetrical "line" dancing is the easiest and most used form of dancing, but it can become tedious after awhile. Try "staging" entrances and exits from different corners. There are no rules!

Combinations Examples

Level 1

4 hip walks, pivot turn, jazz square, lindy, chaíné, touch, 4 hips, grapevine, Vegas walk, fan kick, step, high L kick, cross, prepare, outside pirouette, jazz jump.

Level 2

Chassé, side pas de bourrée, kick ball change, pivot turn, ball change, pivot turn, ball change in second, ball change cross over, chassé, pas de bourrée, double pirouette lunge, lunge, cross kick cross, passé, jazz square, 4 hips, kick front to squat.

Cross ball change, cross ball change, small jeté, spiral turn and point, cross kick, cross lunge, chaíné, turn, drop to ground, roll over to knees, arabesque jump, jazz run offstage.

Level 3

Chaíné, second, pas de bourrée, passé down, pas de bourrée, two pirouettes, lunge, lunge, rotate hinge, 3 walks, passé to ground, swastika attitude, seat spin, rise to standing, arch up and pose.

Always check your choreography. Do you have a balanced routine? Are there:

Rising movements?

Descending movements?

Inward movements?

Outward movements?

Continuous movements?

Abrupt movements?

Symmetrical movements?

Asymmetrical successions?

Directional changes?

Body waves or contractions?

Holds or balances?

Accents?

Gymnastics or mime?

Do not feel it is necessary to include all, but there should be enough variety to complete the picture. Are all transitions smooth especially between turns, jumps, and locomotor moves? How is your use of time? (You may want to always dance "on" the beat.) Did you give resting points or breathing points so the dancers do not sound like a train engine huffing and puffing through the routine? Is there anything original or exciting about your routine? Does the overall dance fit your group's personality and age level? Can you add or take away from the choreographed piece with costuming, lighting, or props? Remember, the parts that will linger in the audience's minds more than anything else in the routine are the beginning and the end.

Staging Directions

Audience

Downstage

Stage Left   Center Stage   Stage Right

Upstage

Backstage

Staging Directions

Upstage. Area of stage away from audience.

Downstage. Area of stage nearest audience.

Stage Right. Dancer's right when facing audience.

Stage Left. Dancer's left when facing audience.

4. Improvisation.   Subconscious related improvisation is one of the best ways to create. This means composing or inventing on the spur of the moment. Improvisation is a chance to express and experiment with not only your own body, but music, rhythm, space, concepts, and emotions. Put yourself into a room or studio alone (preferably with the door locked), turn on some music and let your body go! Quiet your conscious and let your subconscious (feelings and emotions) let go naturally. You will be surprised at your creative ingenuity! Occasionally envision an audience and try to create for them. Improvisation is not only a great way to develop your own style of choreography, but also an excellent aid to help you handle the situation of a "black-out" occurring during a performance. It is something all of us can do occasionally to get out of the structured world.

5. Putting It All Together.   Look at your dance routine as a whole. It is easy to get wrapped up in each individual fragment. Title your piece so that you make sure the title adequately reflects the idea of the work. Is the element of time correct for the piece? (A three-hour dance piece can be a little long for the audience!) Is your routine well rehearsed? Sometimes the easiest routine executed perfectly can be the best routine. Lastly, perform it. The next chapter will show you how!

9 NOW DANCE IT!

Dance, like any art form, is first and foremost a means of self-expression, communication using your body. Dance is also *performed* for the purpose of entertaining the audience. Jazz is a passionate art form that encompassés a full range of feelings and emotions, not just kicks and turns. Feelings can be communicated easily through body movements, so why not release your inner feelings and enjoy! When dance is performed without feeling, it does little for the audience, and if you do not feel the dance yourself, you're missing out on the greatest part of dancing! The inner experience will come to you if you let it. But "how," you ask?

One of the most difficult obstacles for jazz dancers, especially for beginners, is to forget their self-consciousness and "let go." As a novice, or even an advanced student, you probably feel some negative emotions getting in your way, for example, nervous tension,

anxiety, or maybe low self-esteem. How can you get rid of these psychological barriers?

It takes training—a form of mental training that you must develop just as you physically train your body to develop a muscle. It is the same form of training professional athletes use. Just as an athlete is psyched into a competition so must a dancer prepare for a performance. For some, psychological training is more necessary than physical training.

If you are a perfectionist, intimidated by others, overassertive, super sensitive, insecure, overconfident, a nervous wreck or even an "iceberg," your performance may be affected. These types of behavior are all extreme emotional characteristics. Perhaps you are an individual who unfairly places psychological pressures on yourself. For example, you may make unjust comparisons between yourself and dancers whose motivations and talents are on a level you can never reach.

People often make such comparisons simply on performance, leaving out all other reasons, such as health, economics, geographic location, family, training, etc.

Misdirected or unbridled emotions often result in psychological pressures on dancers, which in turn may result in problems with your physical performance. Emotions affect every cell in your body. Your mind and body are intertwined. They are totally connected. Try not to compromise your capabilities with misplaced emotions. This pressure causes anxiety and is manifested in body tension. Anxiety, although normal, can be a distraction that can hinder performance, ruin judgment, and even make you sick. You may never get over the tension, but you can learn how to channel it to aid in a better performance. Everyone seems to feel that pressures and self-doubts are their own dark secrets, but even good dancers have such issues. They really do. They just know how to handle them. Remember, the biggest anxiety producer is you.

Let's generalize how you can better channel your energies in more positive ways. Self-awareness is the first step towards being in better control of your dancing. Become aware of your body and mind by tuning in to your feelings and emotions. Then put yourself in a relaxed state of both mind and body by letting go and breathing deeply and easily. You will concentrate best when you reach *your* optimum level of relaxation (not *too* relaxed and not *too* tense). In dancing concentration is generally more difficult than in ordinary circumstances, because it is usually done under the pressure of performance.

At all times remain focused on the task at hand. Your mind pays attention to only one thing at a time, it will tend to push out things which you were trying to concentrate on. Furthermore, the feelings these emotions engender tend to be more compelling to your imagination than the cool, rational action on which you had intended to focus your attention.

Concentration for the purpose of a dance performance collectively refers to the instructions you give yourself in the form of images (of your routine). As stated previously, if you successfully focus yourself while doing your routine, negative emotions will not have a chance to interfere. This action is called mental rehearsal. It involves you imagining yourself making your dance moves. The more vivid and detailed the visualization (what it looks like, what it sounds like, and what it feels like) the better your body can understand what it has to do. This mental rehearsal makes psyching a habit—your reactions are automatic and there is no need to think. This is one reason why just watching someone dance well can improve the quality of your own performance.

Perhaps you can recall positive moments when everything seems to click (what experts call a flow). Probably the major element that you would recall is that you were *totally* involved in what you were doing . . . unaware of yourself as the doer—aware only of the completed dance. These high moments have four qualities: 1) you are physically free and unhampered by tension 2) you are mentally focused (in the here and now) 3) you are in harmony with your body and mind and 4) you are enjoying it—it feels right. This is the state that you want to reach. The state of flow will be personalized to your style. When a dancer totally commits every aspect of him/herself to the movement, including energy, focus, facial expression, and intent, while remaining true to the character or situation the choreographer has created, a personal style is developed.

Mental rehearsal is not to be confused with wishful thinking or even positive thinking. Wishful thinking is fantasizing about something you hope is coming true but over which you have little control. Positive thinking is telling yourself you can do it. Both are concerned with ends rather than means. With mental rehearsal you are thinking and practicing the means by which you will give your best performance.

Some professional dance troupes have what they call a "green room" before a performance where their sole purpose is to get "centered" for their show. Everyone has their own little way to help them get ready for a production. Some people just need to be by themselves before a show. Whatever it takes, mental preparation is a good idea if you want to perform well and enjoy the meaningful inner experience. So practice mentally as well as physically. Now DANCE IT!

Imagery Techniques:

1. Use **internal vision** as you would see your performance through your own eyes.

2. Use **external vision** as you would see yourself from the teacher's eye or the audiences eye.

3. Visualization works best when you are **relaxed.**

4. **Replay** your best performances.

5. **Preplay** your ideal performance.

6. Strive for **clear, detailed** pictures.

7. **Hear, feel,** and **see** your experience.

8. **Believe** in those pictures. Have confidence.

9. Bring in your spirit. **Let's do it!**

"To dance is to feel ... learn ... love ... express."

10
S-T-R-E-T-C-H-ABILITY

How do you rate on stretching knowledge? Let's take a short self-evaluation test: Select the best answer(s).

1. **What are some good reasons to stretch?**
   a. increase flexibility
   b. increase performance
   c. prevent injuries
   d. relieve tension

2. **How long should I hold a stretch?**
   a. 10 seconds
   b. 15 seconds
   c. 30 seconds
   d. 1 minute
   e. 1 ° minutes

3. **What are the most essential muscles to stretch to prevent posture problems and help with the dancer's center?**
   a. upper back
   b. lower back
   c. hip flexors
   d. quads
   e. calves

4. **How many times per week should I stretch to maintain present flexibility levels?**
   a. once
   b. twice
   c. three
   d. four
   e. five or more

5. **What are the best muscle stretches for doing the splits?**
   a. calves
   b. hamstrings
   c. hip flexors
   d. quads
   e. b and c

6. **How hard should I stretch?**
   a. tingling sensation
   b. slight discomfort
   c. just before the point of pain
   d. burning sensation
   e. no pain

The answers are:

1. a, b, c, d: The most important reason for you to stretch is to prevent problems (injuries) before they happen but each choice is correct.

2. c, d: Most research has shown that optimal benefits are gained for dancers/athletes by holding a stretch for 30-60 seconds.

3. c: One of the most critical muscle groups to prevent forward pelvic tilt (and lower back problems) are the hip flexors. These are normally strong and tight from dance and daily movements like walking.

4. b: A minimum of two stretching sessions per week are needed to maintain and three to four times to improve flexibility.

5. e: The most important muscles to stretch as a beginning step in carrying out an advanced stretch position like the splits are the hamstrings and hip flexors.

6. b, c: Stretching is a relaxing slow process that should stress the muscle/tendon only to the point of pain. There should be slight discomfort.

How did you do? Rate yourself on the following scale:

5 or 6   Ready to take on the world!
4   Expert in the making!
3   Going in the right direction.
2 or 1   Dangerous to yourself and others.

If I were given the choice of being strong or flexible, I would choose being flexible. It is much easier to do repetitive strength exercises than to have to sustain a stretch for thirty seconds and "grin and bear it." However, a balance of both is your best bet as a dancer.

Flexibility is an absolute necessity in dance. The extended ranges of motion which are vital to high level choreography could be considered a severe problem if they were found in an average person without the strength to control it. Did you know muscles can be stretched 150 percent of their normal length?

Why is stretch so important in dance? First it is a means of improving movement and technique. You can't master a skill in dance without being flexible enough to attain the skill. Let's take, for example, a grand battement. How can you stand and practice controlling your kicks to your ears when you do not even have the flexibility to get your leg there in the first place? Increasing flexibility so that your joints can move through a full range of motion with minimum restriction will add to the movement potential of dancers. Movement is the key factor to success in dancing. Flexibility is essential for complete motion. Thus, greater flexibility can allow you to perform more complex dance skills and add more variety to your routines.

Second, flexibility is your biggest safeguard against joint and muscle injury. Injuries to the soft tissues of your muscles are the most common and recurring types of injuries to dancers. Injuries will be less severe, and your recovery time quicker, if you utilize an effective stretching program.

Besides guarding against injury, a third reason for stretching is that it reduces muscle soreness. Muscle soreness can be the result of over-exertion, inadequate conditioning, or over conditioning. Muscle soreness that occurs immediately after exercise will usually subside after short periods of rest. But soreness that persists over a long period of time is of serious concern. This can be a result of spasms in an exercised muscle that has become fatigued and is unable to achieve complete relaxation. Stretching exercises are very effective in preventing such spasms, especially if done *after* a workout.

Let's look at some basic guidelines for stretching. Dancers should always stretch before and after each workout. Recent studies show the greatest flexibility benefits occur due to stretching done during cool down.

Cool down is a crucial time to work out the stiffness created in a hard workout.

Several stretching questions are answered by the FIT principle. This acronym answers how often, how hard, and how long we should stretch. The guidelines are:

F: **Frequency.** Optimal increases happen when a dancer stretches from three to four times a week. Twice a week maintains flexibility levels, but once a week will decrease range of motion.

I: **Intensity.** Proceed to the position desired but only to the point of tightness, then hold with no bouncing. This coaxes your muscle to relax. No strain should be put on your joint. Proper breathing and a relaxed state of mind polish your process.

T: **Time.** Hold each stretch a minimum of 15 seconds and preferably up to 60 seconds. A good technique to measure your time is five deep breathes for every fifteen-second period. Breathe deeply and exhale slowly.

Contracting your muscles before stretching is another way to enhance stretching. This contract-relax method is especially helpful in problem areas or in large muscle groups like hamstrings. You may also want to pay attention to the order in which you stretch. For example stretching calves before proceeding to hamstrings may make hamstring stretches easier.

Warm up and cool down stretches should be preceded and followed by range of motion exercises. Slow resisted exercises might add to the effectiveness of warm up or cool down.

The muscles of the body have a natural tendency to shorten with age. Observe the stiffness of many elderly people. This is due to changes in tissue as well as lower level of activity. It is never too late to start stretching properly. Gentle stretching can counteract the tendency towards aging stiffness.

Remember to stretch your mind before you stretch your body. Stretch before and after workout with emphasis on cool down to increase flexibility, prevent injuries and lessen workout stiffness. Dancers should develop a "sixth sense" of movement and listen to their bodies. If a muscle or an area feels particularly tight, it should be stretched longer. "Know yourself" is the watch phrase. Don't bounce, tug, or push at the point of pain. A movement required for a special dance move needs extra attention. Many people don't notice an increase in flexibility for several weeks. It is your responsibility to stay safe and flexible, if class does not give you enough time to warm up or cool down, spend the time yourself.

The combination of greater extension, easier movements, better movement potential, and less susceptibility to injury and soreness will keep you dancing longer with stronger performances. Be sure to develop and carry out your own program so that you too can create the habit of stretching for life.

11 THE DANCER AS AN ATHLETE

Have you ever wondered what happens to former jazz dancers in their later years? Are they healthy or more healthy than the normal population? How well are you?

I was compelled to write this chapter because in my travels I have encountered many wonderfully talented former dancers who are permanently injured. Many have suffered from chronic pain, malnutrition and burnout due to inaccurate advice and insufficient training. Why is it that dancers who are so dependent on their bodies abuse them so much? After many inquiries, I discovered that it basically boiled down to two reasons, lack of knowledge and lack of self-responsibility. This chapter very briefly covers both of these areas. I urge you to further your readings in any of the following areas that are of interest to you.

Being involved as a student and teacher in both dance and athletics, I observed a lot of similarity between both fields. It is apparent that as well as being accomplished artists, dancers are superb athletes. Both endeavors require enormous energy. Student dancers and dance teachers must do everything in their power to take care of their bodies. Fortunately, it is not that difficult.

Just as an athlete can benefit from some good solid dance training for body awareness, and coordination and suppleness in their sport, dancers can also benefit from proper conditioning, nutritional awareness, injury prevention and treatment, cardiovascular training, and relaxation techniques. Approaching life from a wholeness perspective and using moderation and balance, are good guidelines to remember.

The areas in which you may want to check yourself for a higher level of wellness and performance are:

1. ***Self-Responsibility.*** This is probably the most important area on this list. An active sense of accountability for yourself and your condition is the necessary motivation to lead a better lifestyle. The greatest cause of poor health in dancers is that most of them neglect themselves or leave the maintenance of their health to others. As a dancer your body is your instrument so you must take care of it— no one else will. This means deciding for yourself how dedicated to your own health you will be. Hints for better health include nutrition, balanced strength and flexibility, cardiovascular training, and mental conditioning. These are keys to having a long, healthy, serious dancing career.

2. ***Balanced Strength and Flexibility Program.*** While almost all dancers readily recognize the importance of flexibility, and they take steps to ensure that the musculature surrounding their joints is supple (and thereby flexible), far fewer dancers accept the fact that they must develop adequate levels of strength if they are to safely sustain their performance levels. Increasing the strength of the musculature surrounding a joint decreases the likelihood that a joint will ever suffer an injury. Remember, an ounce of prevention is worth a pound of cure. How unfortunate it would be for you to be sidelined from an activity you love (jazz dancing) because of an injury that might have been prevented. Developing a *balanced* strength and flexibility program can not always be accomplished in dance class. Conditioning outside of class work gives you an opportunity to keep muscles balanced, strong, and supple.

For example a key to minimizing or totally preventing lower back problems is to engage in a properly developed muscular fitness (strength) program. It is widely known that one of the nation's major health problems is lower back pain and lower back injuries. In many instances these back ailments are the result of postural misalignment. Such ailments are often caused by a lack of adequate strength in the muscles surrounding the skeletal joints of the lower back or by an imbalance in the strength level between the antagonistic muscle groups of the lower back and abdominal region. The muscles of the lower back and the abdominal area should be approximately equal in strength. When abdominal muscles increase in strength without corresponding increase in strength by the lower back muscles, lower back discomfort will often result.

3. ***Cardiovascular Exercise.*** Depending upon their personal programs, some dancers do not receive sufficient aerobic benefits from their dance workouts. Because of the "stop and go" process of their dance workouts cardiovascular systems in dancers are often not stressed to a point where improvement can occur. Since a healthy heart is the core of a physically fit lifestyle, it would be advantageous for almost all dancers to engage in aerobic-type exercises in addition to dancing. Examples of activities that will develop your cardiovascular system include swimming, aerobic dancing, walking, jogging, cycling, cross-country skiing and rowing. It is suggested that an aerobic activity be performed for fifteen minutes continuously, at least three times a week, *within* your training heart zone (remember to allow time to get your heart in the training heart zone and allow for a proper cool down). If you

select aerobic dancing as your developmental cardiovascular activity you should be aware that even though quite a few jazz movements are used in aerobic dancing, they are usually danced in "freeform" (not emphasizing technique). The main purpose of the movements in aerobic dancing is to get the heart rate going. Aerobic dancing is an excellent activity for a jazz dancer just to "let go" and "have fun" as long as the dancer can resume control of his/her movements at any time. You should remember, before engaging in any aerobic activity, to take your pulse and check the charts on your minimum and maximum heart rates for the activity. Aerobic exercise, combined with a low-fat diet and no smoking is the best way to take care of your cardiovascular system.

Age	Training Heart Rates Based on Percentage of Predicted Maximum Heart Rate and 10-Second Counts			
	70%	75%	80%	85%
15 – 19	23	25	27	28
20 – 29	23	24	26	28
30 – 39	22	23	25	26
40 – 49	20	22	23	25
50 – 59	19	21	22	23
60 – 70	18	19	21	22
> 70	17	18	19	21

Target Heart Rate Chart

4. ***Diet and Nutrition.*** Diet and proper nutrition can play a vital role in your performance. Despite the controversy surrounding nutrition, most authorities agree on the following common denominators in a proper diet:

1. Eat fruits and vegetables daily.

2. Eat high fiber, such as whole grains, daily.

3. For protein sources stay with lean products such as poultry, fish, beans and legumes.

4. Avoid fats and refined sugar as much as possible.

5. Do not be "afraid" of carbohydrates.

As a dancer, it would be to your advantage to eat six small meals a day. Eating small meals during the day will keep your glucose level in balance. By adding water to juice, you will reduce your glucose fluctuation. Small, healthy snacks during rehearsal are suggested to keep your energy level up. It is advisable not to eat one hour before taking class. Do not skip meals or change your diet prior to a performance (i.e. carbohydrate load). The best meal before a performance is complex carbohydrates eaten approximately three hours before you plan to exert yourself.

Watch your fat intake as well as your calorie intake. High levels of fat reduce metabolism and can make you tired. The "inside" of your body is as important as the outside. Consult experts to determine your idea body fat percentage. The recommended levels for dancers are 10% or less for men, and less than 20% for women but women need to be careful if your fat percentage is below ten percent. If you eat a balanced diet with sufficient amounts of each of the basic food groups you do not need to ingest any food or vitamin supplements. There have been numerous studies that have conclusively documented the fact that for a person *who eats a balanced diet* such supplements may be a waste of money. Supplement your diet only according to your needs. It also has been widely documented that drugs, alcohol, and caffeine are counterproductive to the health of a dancer. Water is the most essential nutrient for your body. Do drink, drink, drink, that wonderful H$_2$O! Water makes all the systems in the body function better.

5. *Mental Conditioning.* As mentioned previously, training and performing involve more than physical aspects of the activity, they also require adherence to the "mental" side of dancing. Read the chapter "Now Dance It" to learn how to better cope with performing pressures. By controlling your mind (which takes practice) you can gain absolute control over your body. You can learn how to make proper use of emotional energy. You can then discover that mental training is practice in the art of living—a way of life. Enjoyment rather than compulsive achievement is the best principal of training. Ninety-eight percent of your dance life is spent training, practicing and rehearsing, so learn to enjoy the process of training itself.

To "psyche" is to be worry free, calm, and alert, and to get the most out of the dancing physically, mentally, and emotionally. Learn how to both tolerate and give criticism. Learn how to set and accomplish short- and long-term goals. The effort of visualization—mentally practicing what you want to achieve—is an effective aid to competition and preparation. Visualize with pictures, feelings and words, the roles you want to play.

Sometimes dance students and teachers can get "hyper." As you develop your energy to a certain level stay in control of it. If you are unable to relax outside dancing you may want to take courses in stress management and/or meditation. Inner peace is a goal that can help anyone in all aspects of his/her life.

6. *Stay active if you decide to finish your dancing career.* Lack of exercise can lead to premature bodily aging. The results can be manifested by infirmity, feebleness, frailness, and low-energy levels. If you end your dancing career, keep dance or some other athletic activity as a recreational hobby. Some of the physiological benefits of staying active are low blood pressure, reduced body fat levels, increased endorphine levels, and a better support for your skeletal structure. Staying active can also give you greater self-confidence and an increased ability to manage stress. Or better yet, keep dancing! You have selected a wonderful art form of physical, mental, social, emotional, and spiritual exercise!

12 FOR TEACHERS ONLY

If you are a teacher of jazz dance you are in an exciting occupation. You have a job that helps others in a creative and exciting world of entertainment. You will meet all types of wonderful people while challenging yourself physically and mentally.

The following questions are frequently asked by teachers like yourself. Remember, you are not alone!

Q. *How can I motivate my students?*
A. Enthusiasm or lethargy can be contagious. The teacher's own enthusiasm for dance and the day's procedures are essential to any well-motivated class. Be aware of your own voice and eye contact. Change tone and pitch to maintain interest. Use appropriate gestures in moderation.

Students work more willingly for a teacher they like. Take pains to humanize yourself to students by sharing facts about your interests, family, or various anecdotes. Friendliness is always appreciated but be careful of too much familiarity. Teachers should never strive to be comedians, but a smile or a laugh never hurt anyone. The class that laughs together works together.

Every time you begin class, try giving the students a word, phrase or idea to concentrate on. For example "Let's begin class by focusing on breathing," then describe the breathing process. This also works well with short term goals such as "Let's really concentrate on the arms today and their importance in turning because we will be working on triple pirouettes."

Do not let students sit in class or socialize during class. They can be taught respect. You could tell them they can drop when you do! Try using students to help with attendance or demonstrations during class.

Variety is the spice of dance classes. Change lesson plans to incorporate new ideas and vary established concepts. Change your music as much as time allows and have students change their orientation of space in class by taking them away from the mirror during the warm up exercises. Another way to change the students class space is to have them go from corner to corner rather than side to side when performing locomotor movements. When performing combinations, divide the students into groups so they can perform for each other. You may want to use this idea just for the more advanced students. For fun and challenge, speed up the tempo of the routine they are performing.

Maintain a good working environment, which includes proper temperature, light, and ventilation. Neatness sets an example of orderliness and efficiency. Use inspirational posters or bulletin boards with worthwhile ideas/images.

Q. *My dance background is limited. Is it necessary that I demonstrate every movement to my students?*
A. There are two types of teachers, the action-oriented and the analytical. In the chapter "Now Dance It" I mentioned briefly the advantages of students who learn through watching (i.e., automatic reaction and more vivid mental images). I personally have never studied under anyone who could not perform what they were instructing. I feel it would be to your advantage to train as much as possible yourself. However, there are those who, because of physical and training limitations, have taught successfully by verbal explanation. For those teachers I recommend that you enforce "mental images" by encouraging students to observe performances, films, television productions, and books. Do not be afraid to single out a few of your best students to demonstrate. This will help instill a feeling of accomplishment and pride in them. Lastly, if you do not have an extensive dance background, do not feel intimidated. Instead, grasp all you can and pass it on to your students. Give them direction that will further enrich their studies.

Q. *My facility is limited. How can I teach different ability levels in one class?*
A. A very good question and probably one of the hardest to answer. Unfortunately, due to economic conditions, many studios and schools are faced with a limited amount of time and thus, must resort to combining classes.

Your best solution would be to keep the advanced classes small by enlarging the beginning level classes. At the beginning stage, students are experiencing and experimenting with their bodies often for the first time, and do not need as much individual attention. In fact, in larger classes, the novice may feel less inhibited because he/she can get "lost in the crowd."

Try making the intermediate level a "technique only" class. You can hold auditions for the more advanced levels. Of course, if they are all in one class, adapt the choreography and speed of the routine to accommodate the different abilities. For example, beginners perform a grapevine to the left, while intermediate dancers perform a chaîné to the left, and advanced dancers could perform two chaîné turns to the left, all during the same part of the combination. Divide them into their ability groups and have beginners practice dancing the combination to a slower beat per minute than intermediate dancers, and have intermediate dancers perform to a slower beat per minute than advanced dancers.

Q. *At what age should you learn jazz?*
A. Any age! Because of the natural body positions there is not as much danger to the body as other dance forms, such as ballet. I know three year olds who just love it! Obviously you must be aware of what types of movements to teach younger and older

students. I would not advise teaching sensuous jazz movements to a six-year old! Of course their memory retention is less, so you would want to repeat moves more, be careful of the strength and stretching exercises you use and play music they can relate to. Younger students like rhythm, and jazz dancing is a great way to expose them to it.

Q. *Some of my students have danced and outgrown my teaching. Where do they go from here?*

A. It takes an unselfish and wise teacher to ask that question. If the student is quite good and desires to continue on a career of dancing, encourage him/her to study at the nearest professional studio. It would be an asset to inform him/her what a dancing career involves (possible change in geographic location, financial pressures, etc.) If the student desires to dance for recreational purposes, have him/her assist in the group's choreography. One can always "grow" in the area of choreography and instruction.

Q. *Which is the best teaching method for my class—records, tapes, musicians, or no music at all?*

A. This is a matter of personal preference. Some teachers use musicians or no music (finger clicking and counting) because they want to stop and correct frequently. Having a drummer, conga player or pianist can be an advantage providing they play to the rhythm you desire and keep an inspired melody. Others prefer a personalized taped cassette of continuous music to keep the movement going so that a good warm-up of the body occurs. The most economical method is to use audio cassettes. Compact discs are becoming more prominent in the studios, but are also more expensive. Phonograph records are still being used by instructors who cannot find the music they desire in any other format. By changing your music frequently, not only are you keeping updated, but it can be a motivating factor for your classes.

Q. *How can I popularize and expand my program?*

A. The best exposure and publicity for your program is to start a performing dance group. This is a great way to get community support and is the least expensive type of publicity. It is also a chance for your dancers to get more involved with the program. There are various dance competitions they can enter to give them goals to strive for. But, be aware of the expense of travelling, costumes, and music before embarking on this project.

Q. *I live in an isolated town and could use some new ideas for choreography and instruction. Where should I go?*

A. Besides reading literature on the subject, there are numerous films and videos distributed by dance suppliers. Another idea is to hire master teachers to teach at your studio. Of course, dance conventions and caravans are extremely beneficial, but be selective. There are many privately operated conventions and caravans that can charge enormous sums of money for less than qualified instruction. However, it is one of the best means of meeting others in your field and sharing ideas. Camps that last one or more weeks are also a great way to learn because there is more time for extensive training. Again, I stress inquiring into them first and consulting people who have attended them previously. I have attended and taught at numerous camps and workshops myself and have sometimes observed the staff setting very bad examples. I have also seen unfair student-teacher ratios. I do not want to discourage you because the workshops can be extremely beneficial. Just be sure the staff if qualified! Of course, traveling to Los Angeles or the Big Apple is always an exciting way to learn!

Q. *I am a small college (or high school) physical education instructor and would love to begin a dance program in my school. Could you give me some guidelines?*

A. More and more jazz dance classes are being offered in the school systems and I think that is wonderful! In order for us to keep jazz dance at a high standard, here are some guidelines:

1. You must be qualified. A major in dance education combined with professional studio instruction is probably your best preparation. Attend a dance workshop where you can self-assess your capabilities to determine if you are qualified.

2. Present a tally of student interest and a report of the values of offering a dance program to your administration. The report should illustrate the many valuable contributions of dance education. You may want to include not only its physical benefits, but its theatrical, social, artistic, recreational, therapeutic, aesthetic, and individual benefits as well.

3. Plan out the financial backing, personnel and facility. Take these three aspects into consideration for the future or your successful dance program could come to a screaming halt! Most of your expenses will come from performing (costumes, props, lighting) and hiring qualified personnel. Do not sacrifice your body to a concrete or extremely slippery floor for lack of another facility.

Q. *I teach in a situation where I am only allotted 45 minutes to teach. How can I successfully teach in that time frame?*
A. Talk to your administration about lengthening it to either one or one and one-half hours!! Assuming you have already tried that, and since something is better than nothing, here are some suggestions.

Try spending twenty minutes on exercise technique, five minutes on turns, ten minutes on locomotive movement, and the remainder on combinations or routines. The movements you use in the exercise and locomotor sections can be used in the combinations (routine). A very useful approach would be to concentrate on one technique a week (for example turns, walks, leaps, or spotting) and make it the execution priority for each class held during that week.

Q. *How can I grade my students on a creative art?*
A. Identify specific objectives for students to reach. One idea would be to grade more on the execution of specific technique skills rather than on the student's natural or unnatural rhythm. Avoid grading beginning students on choreography because they must learn their techniques first and their creative use of dance movements will be limited. Try grading by using the jazz syllabus which lists levels of specific dance techniques the students must master before advancing.

Best wishes . . . . be well . . . good luck . . . . let's do it!

For more information regarding Christy Lane's jazz dance videos, syllabus cards, syllabus worksheets, and workshops please contact:

Let's Do It! Productions
P.O. Box 5483
Spokane, WA 99205
(509) 235-6555

*Note: All jazz dance techniques taught in this book are available on video.

All bodywear and footwear in this book has been supplied by Capezio-Ballet Makers, Inc. For a catalog contact:

Capezio-Ballet Makers, Inc.
Promotional Department
1411 Broadway
New York, NY 10019
(212) 354-1887

INDEX